UNIQUE EATS AND EATERIES

OF THE

TWIN CITIES

TERRI PETERSON SMITH

Library of Congress Control Number: 2017934682

ISBN: 9781681061108

Printed in the United States of America

17 18 19 20 21   5 4 3 2 1

All photo credits belong to author unless otherwise noted.

Photo Credits page 1:

First row right, Courtney Perry

Second row right, Tongue in Cheek

Fourth row left, The Sioux Chef

DEDICATION

To my dining companions and fellow culinary explorers who helped with research for this book: Scott Smith, Mary Linstroth, Len and Martha Rice, Ron and Leslie Steubs, Jim Brandeberry, Shea Smith, Katie Moran, and Cathy Liebman.

CONTENTS

INTRODUCTION

This is a guide to ninety of the most interesting restaurants in Minneapolis and St. Paul—Minnesota's fraternal "twins" separated by the Mississippi River. It's no easy task to select only ninety from a dining scene that is regularly described by regional and national media as "white hot" and "America's next great food city," and many more deserving eateries are located in this area. Twin Cities chefs, blessed in part by the fresh abundance from nearby farms and lakes, annually receive a great many nominations for James Beard Foundation awards, and new eateries enter the market at an astounding pace. What fun it is to sample and narrow down such an extraordinary list!

All but one of these eateries fall within the city limits of Minneapolis and St. Paul, and the one outlier absolutely merits a short trip to a nearby burb. All have staying power in an industry where establishments come and go rapidly, and they represent a cross-section of the food experiences available in the Twin Cities, ranging from supersophisticated and stylish eats to homey comfort food, from hard-core carnivorous to vegan, from ethnic to all-American, and from beloved local classics to the trendiest dining darlings. Good food is what's essential, but each of these eateries serves up an interesting experience with creativity, humor, and a dose of history, too. You'll even find places that will teach you how to whip up your own special meals. The resulting list adds up to a view of the spirit and attitude of the Twin Cities through the lens of food.

Ultimately, *Unique Eats and Eateries: Twin Cities* isn't just about eating; it's about exploration. The thriving, laid-back neighborhood eateries make perfect starting points for food-based investigations of each city that reveal the fascinating history and the many cultures that define us. Among these eateries, diners may trace the Cities' food roots back to the Native Americans who hunted game and harvested wild rice from local lakes and rivers. Since then, each new wave of settlers and immigrants—Scandinavians, the Irish, Germans, Eastern Europeans, the Vietnamese, the Hmong, Koreans, Somalis, Hispanics—have added their particular traditions to the mix and spiced up life in the Twin Cities far beyond what one might expect in the Midwest. Most importantly, in an era when people tend to huddle close to home with like-minded folks, restaurants provide one of the few ways to interact and get acquainted with fellow citizens who are very different from us and in neighborhoods that aren't typically on our radar. As Chef Lachelle Cunningham of Breaking Bread Café put it, "Food offers one of the best ways for people to connect, let their guards down, break bread, and break down barriers."

Whether you're new to the area or Twin Cities born and bred, use this book to launch your own exploration and travel to these eateries in the spirit of a mini road trip. While you're in the neighborhood, create your own list of favorite eateries, shops, and entertainment venues and spread the word. Bon appétit and bon voyage!

UNIQUE EATS AND EATERIES

OF THE

TWIN CITIES

112 EATERY

Wedged into a small Warehouse District storefront, 112 Eatery showcases everything a great restaurant ought to offer—creative gourmet cuisine, an outstanding wine card, and spot-on service in a chic, comfortable setting, all without breaking the bank. Small wonder that 112 Eatery is one of Minneapolis's finest and most popular dining destinations, perfect for romantic evenings, business tête-à-têtes, birthday and anniversary celebrations, late nights on the town, and everything in between.

To describe 112's menu, crafted by James Beard Foundation award-winning chef Isaac Becker, as eclectic is an understatement. Global tastes merge and meld among such delicious offerings as the foie gras and lardon salad, blue prawns with serrano chili mayonnaise, nori-encrusted sirloin with tangy citrus/soy sauce, duck pate banh mi, stringozzi pasta with lamb sugo, tagliatelle noodles with foie gras meatballs, and baby lamb ribs with fish-sauce caramel and assorted Japanese spices. More domestically inclined palates will fall for 112's bacon, egg, and harissa sandwich; a delectable brie-topped cheeseburger; and its legendary steak tartare. While all the desserts are terrific, Nancy Silverton's butterscotch budino may be the finest sweet-and-salty delight on the planet. The wine list is equally outstanding and, for a restaurant of 112's quality, happily well priced.

Indeed, 112's core philosophy centers on the notion of accessibility to great food and drink for diners of all stripes and pocketbooks. Most menu items are priced below twenty dollars, and a cost-conscious couple can enjoy a satisfying dinner of appetizer, entrée, dessert, and wine for a hundred dollars without self-denial. The interior is cozy and unpretentious, an easygoing bistro where jeans and business suits are equally at home. Its late-night hours—112's full kitchen is open until midnight Monday through Thursday and to 1:00 a.m. on Fridays and Saturdays—attract throngs of Uptown and North Loop hipsters and fashionistas, post-theatergoers, young urban professionals, and even chefs and staff from other establishments suffering from a

Top right: Duck pate banh mi sandwich is a casual favorite at 112 Eatery.

Above left: Crafting cocktails at the 112 bar.

Above right: Beet and blood orange salad at 112 Eatery.

case of the gourmet munchies.

Given all this, it's no surprise that 112 Eatery has been featured by the *New York Times, Bon Appetit, GQ,* and dozens of other reviewers as one of Minneapolis's top restaurants. Reservations are a necessity, although patient, impromptu singles and pairs can often snag a seat at the bar. 112 also offers a private dining room for up to sixteen people. Street, pay lot, and ramp parking are available in the area.

112 N. Third St., Minneapolis
612-343-7696
112eatery.com

ALMA

Don't mention the maxim "if it ain't broke, don't fix it" to James Beard Award-winning chef Alex Roberts. After sixteen-plus uninterrupted years of culinary brilliance at his acclaimed Restaurant Alma, in 2016 Roberts completely reconfigured his restaurant, an adjoining coffee shop, and upstairs space into a university-area gem: a sleek and intimate restaurant, a lively café and bar, and a cozy seven-room boutique hotel. The critics haven't stopped raving since.

Alma's dinner-only restaurant features a three-course, prix fixe epicurean experience, with five modern American dishes to choose from in each course. First-course favorites include a bitter greens salad with goat cheese, dates, and avocado and anchovy vinaigrette; soft egg and caviar atop potato puree with black-truffle vinaigrette; and bison tartare with pear and chili aioli. The middle course presents a variety of eclectic pasta and grain dishes, aromatic coconut shellfish stew, and a spicy *masa* crepe with mushrooms, pickled red onions, and chard. Poblano-crusted sturgeon, pan-roasted chicken, seared sea scallops, braised beef, and duck breast make up the entrée choices. All three courses offer vegetarian options. Alma's exceptional wine list and elegant, comfortable dining room complete a sumptuous dining experience for romantic couples, business executives, people celebrating special occasions, or good friends seeking great food and drink.

The Nordic modern café and bar, humming from sunup to sundown and beyond, sparkles with verve and hipness. Fresh-baked croissants, danish, and other goodies from Alma's bakery and classic and innovative egg-and-meat dishes make for a delightful breakfast. Midday diners can choose from a subset of breakfast items; savory sandwiches and burgers; salads and soups; and meat, cheese, and marinated veggie boards perfect for sharing. The café's standout dinner card features small plates; pasta and grain dishes; a clam, chorizo, and white bean stew; other steak, chop, fowl, and seafood entrées; and succulent sides. Or just sit at the café's long, curving bar, sip one of its signature cocktails—perhaps its butternut squash daiquiri, deemed the Twin Cities' Best Drink of 2016 by

Top left: Miso-glazed salmon. Photo by Alma

Top right: Alma cooks work in the open kitchen. Photo by Alma

Mpls. St. Paul Magazine—and watch skilled chefs ply their trade in one of Alma's three gleaming kitchens. Whether you're an out-of-town visitor or a local on an overnight getaway, Alma's chic, comfy lodgings provide the perfect ending to a memorable night out.

Alma accepts reservations for the restaurant and café for parties of five or more. Valet parking is available, and ample area street parking also exists.

528 University Ave. SE, Minneapolis
612-379-4909
almampls.com

AL'S BREAKFAST

It seems appropriate that tiny Al's Breakfast resides in the Dinkytown neighborhood near the University of Minnesota campus. Probably the narrowest restaurant in Minneapolis, Al's is located in a former alleyway, and its fourteen seats have accommodated the behinds of students, alumni, and tourists alike since the 1950s, when the late Al Bergstrom first fired up the griddles. Not much has changed since then, which is why Al's won a James Beard Foundation award in the "America's Classics" category.

Because of its size, diners must observe the protocol: a line forms along the back wall of the café and often out the door. It usually moves fairly quickly because staff members instruct folks when to be seated and when to change seats (even when they're already eating) to accommodate new diners. Still, it's all worth it for Al's eggs Benedict with corned beef, kosher salmon, or mushrooms; huevos rancheros; or omelets with every combination of filling. Pancakes come in just about as many variations—e.g., with walnuts, blueberries, sweet corn, or chocolate chips. Al's Facebook page alerts fans to such daily specials as "crab and shrimp cakes with poached eggs, and stuff." Open 6:00 a.m. (9:00 a.m. on Sundays) to 1:00 p.m. Come hungry, and bring cash or personal checks only.

413 Fourteenth Ave. SE, Minneapolis
612-331-9991
alsbreakfastmpls.com

Top: Tiny Al's Breakfast near the University of Minnesota is an American classic. Photo by Alison Kirwin

Above left: Pancakes and eggs come in just about every imaginable combination and variety. Photo by Alison Kirwin

Above right: Diners eat at fourteen seats along the counter and can watch their order being cooked on the griddle. Photo by Daryl Miller

BABANI'S KURDISH RESTAURANT

Though Minneapolis and St. Paul both teem with large immigrant communities, Kurds form an extremely small slice of the Twin Cities' ethnic population. By some accounts, only twenty to thirty Kurdish families reside in the area. So how does Babani's—proudly proclaiming itself the first Kurdish restaurant in the United States and the only one in the Cities today—thrive among Minnesotans who, when asked about Kurds, likely think first of unprocessed cheese? The short answer is that great food served in a warm, inviting, family-run establishment transcends ethnic labels.

Babani's owes its authentic Kurdish fare to the culinary talents of owner and chef Rodwan Nakshabandi. A survivor of the Iran-Iraq War, Saddam Hussein's genocidal campaign against Iraqi Kurds, and a Kurdish refugee camp in Turkey, Nakshabandi ultimately came to St. Paul after Desert Storm and founded Babani's in 1997. Today, Babani's proudly celebrates Kurdish cuisine, culture, and traditions on the city's west side, just across the river from downtown.

Fans of Mediterranean and Middle Eastern cuisines will feel right at home at Babani's. Its Kurdish staples include Kubay Sawar and Kubay Brinj, two tasty spiced, ground beef–filled dumplings of wheat and rice; Dowjic soup, featuring chicken and rice in a tart lemon and yogurt broth with generous amounts of pepper and oregano; Jaajic salad, a creamy concoction of cucumber, dill, garlic, and yogurt; and the house specialty, Sheik Babani, a wonderful ground beef–stuffed eggplant dish named for its resemblance to pin-striped dress trousers. Babani's also features tabouli, kibbe-style beef and chicken kebabs, and dolmas (seasoned rice-stuffed grape leaves). Moist, delicious Kurdish bread accompanies most entrées. After-meal treats include Turkish coffee, generously infused with cardamom; aromatic Kurdish tea; and Nakshabandi's special Kurdish baklava—moist, firm, chewy and without the syrupy sweetness that often characterizes other pastries of the same name.

The handsome decor also pays homage to Babani's heritage. The central dining room's walls are adorned with beautiful Kurdish rugs,

Top right: Kubay Brinj, rice dumplings filled with ground beef, spices, and parsley fried to a crispy brown.

Above left: Babani's Rodwan Nakshabandi bakes a Kurdish version of baklava.

Above right: Kurdish beef kababs at Babani's.

and lovely Arabian-style lanterns descend from the latticed ceiling. Photographs of Kurdish tribesmen and families and Kurdistan scenery hang throughout. The atmosphere is charming, cozy, and comfortable.

Babani's caters to everyone from well-dressed professionals to local industrial workers, area residents, and families with small children. Closed on Sundays, Babani's accepts reservations for lunch and dinner, and walk-ins are also welcomed but may experience a wait during peak hours. Free parking is available in Babani's large lot immediately adjacent to the restaurant.

32 Fillmore Ave. E., St. Paul
651-602-9964
babanis.com

BETTY DANGER'S COUNTRY CLUB

Billing itself as "a country club for the 99 percent," Betty Danger's takes dead and irreverent aim at the Biff-and-Muffy set, piercing preppiness and high society with low camp and kitsch. The result is a dining and entertainment experience unlike anything else in the Twin Cities.

Let's start with the Mechanical Tree, a.k.a. "the Danger" or the "vertically rotating patio," that dominates the exterior. In reality, it's a fifty-foot-high, pink-and-green Ferris wheel offering patrons a fifteen- to thirty-minute spin while partaking of food and drink. Delightful in the summer, a tad chilly in the winter, the Mechanical Tree runs year-round. On the other side of the clubhouse is perhaps the world's only par 49, 8½ hole miniature golf course, featuring gorillas, camels, wolves, bears, and other mammalian obstacles between tee and green. Adjoining them is a spacious horizontal patio that draws large crowds on summer evenings.

Tongue remains firmly planted in cheek inside Betty's clubhouse, which is divided into two dining rooms roughly separated by a large bar area. The main dining room is decorated in colonial hunt club design and festooned with trophies, "fine" china, and animal mounts. The sunny garden room sports wrought-iron patio furniture and a central fountain and opens onto the horizontal patio in the summer. Hosts and servers are clad in their best preppy plaids and prints (while also adorned with a variety of hair colors and tattoos), and the menus lie within '50s-ish manuals, suggesting, among other things, proper attire and ladylike decorum for club guests.

The fare at Betty Danger's is "Mexampton"—a cross between Mexico and the Hamptons—and includes a variety of taco plates, quesadillas, burritos, and enchiladas, with most providing a fair degree of spiciness. Appetizers abound and can easily be converted into a full meal. Betty's drink card features several different margaritas—named after Ivy League schools, naturally—plus other specialty drinks honoring the *Sporting Life*, a nice selection of craft

Top right: Golf at this "country club" takes place on the world's only par 49, 8½ hole miniature golf course, featuring an animal menagerie. Photo by Betty Danger's Country Club

Above right: Casual country club eats at Betty's include tacos, burritos, and burgers. Photo by Betty Danger's Country Club

Above left: Eat your heart out, ritzy country clubbers. This country club has a Ferris wheel. Photo by Betty Danger's Country Club

beers on tap and in cans/bottles, and red and white wines. Betty's also offers lunch and brunch on Saturdays and Sundays.

Betty's hours vary seasonally, and it is occasionally closed for private events; hence, check the website or call ahead for availability. Reservations are available and highly recommended. Betty's has its own parking lot, though it's often filled to overflowing, and valet parking is also available. Plus, the "Tiki Tram" shuttles patrons between Betty's and her older sister's equally wacky restaurant and bar, Psycho Suzi's Motor Lounge (see page 116) three blocks away, for a small charge.

2501 Marshall St. NE, Minneapolis
612-315-4997
bettydangers.com

BIG DADDY'S BBQ

Ron Whyte and Bob Edmond, the gentlemen behind the grill at Big Daddy's BBQ, have been smoking and roasting meat in the Frogtown neighborhood for more than thirty years. Besides their regular jobs, they began by selling meat barbecued in the open air in parks and under tents on weekends, using recipes and cooking traditions that came from their early days in Kentucky and Georgia. Savory smoke wafted through the neighborhood, and hundreds of barbecue lovers followed their noses to congregate like a big party at their grills.

Bad weather and the health department eventually brought them indoors to a small, sunny café, right on the Dale stop on the Green Line. Motown music provides just the right mood to dine in, or you can carry out their barbecue too. They still offer succulent ribs and chicken and Big Daddy sandwiches of smokehouse pulled pork and chicken. If you're hungry, tackle one of their signature, aptly named Flintstone sandwiches, with beef short rib piled high with their house-made sauce. Great as the meat is at Big Daddy's, the sides are not to be ignored. Choose from the perfectly crunchy coleslaw,

Frogtown is one of St. Paul's oldest and most ethnically diverse neighborhoods. Its curious name dates to around 1860, when its earliest German residents labeled the swampy, lowland area immediately west of downtown, filled with croaking frogs, as Froschburg–Frog City in English. For decades, Frogtown was home to Polish, German, Scandinavian, and Irish immigrants drawn to the area's inexpensive housing, railroad yards, and factories. When the nearby Rondo neighborhood, home to about 85 percent of St. Paul's African-American population, was decimated in the 1960s by the construction of Interstate 94, many Rondo residents relocated to Frogtown.

Left: Big Daddy's BBQ is one of the Twin Cities' favorite barbecue spots.

Right: Got a big appetite? Tuck into one of Big Daddy's Flintstone sandwiches.

mac and cheese, collard greens, and cornbread. And those yummy baked beans ... they have a certain special ingredient (a little extra vinegar?), and no amount of questioning will get the chefs to reveal the secret.

In summer the large patio ties the restaurant back, at least a little, to its outdoor roots. Look for live music here on Fridays and Saturdays.

625 University Ave. W., St. Paul
651-222-2516
bigdaddysbbq-stpaul.com

Over time, with the loss of area blue-collar jobs and the foreclosure crisis, the neighborhood fell on hard times. But a recent influx of Latino, Hmong, and Somali immigrants has brought new business and vitality to the neighborhood, and today Frogtown teems with Asian pho restaurants, halal meat markets, multilingual professional services, and new residential construction along University Avenue's light-rail corridor.

BIRCHWOOD CAFÉ

A Zen quotation hangs over the counter at Birchwood Café: "Innumerable measures bring this food. We should know how it comes to us." That's the concept behind every meal served at this neighborhood restaurant, where the food is beautifully prepared, organic, and served with a side of food-based social justice.

Birchwood Café traces its roots back to 1926, when the site was a dairy. Looking at the neighborhood now, that's hard to imagine. The Bursch family converted the dairy into a neighborhood grocery in the 1940s, selling groceries and serving as a place for folks to meet and swap news. It became the Birchwood Café in 1995 and retains its connection to both locally produced food and the goal of creating community.

Birchwood serves breakfast, weekend brunch, lunch, dinner, and desserts (plus beer, wine, and cocktails). It prides itself on an especially close relationship with its suppliers at organic farms and growers that use sustainable practices. Unlike most of us, it looks at food through a lens of *eight* seasons: spring, summer, scorch, autumn, dusk, frost, winter, and thaw—a way to incorporate in creative ways what's particularly available and fresh from those local farmers. So, for example, in winter, diners may find a roasted roots hand pie with turnip, parsnip, celery root, sweet onions, kale, and feta in cream-cheese pastry, served with sunchoke puree. Savory waffles of kale, quinoa, and feta come with pineapple chutney, lemon rosemary butter, sunflower seeds, bacon lardoons, sunny-side egg, maple syrup, and powdered sugar. Yum. The winter salad delivers kale, meat, and cheese from local producers, midseason oranges, orange champagne vinaigrette, candied cranberries, and sunflower seeds. It's enough to make you like winter.

While you're there, the folks at the Café want to draw your attention (and maybe your participation) to food-related issues, such as human and environmental health, climate change, and social justice. That's why they launched Birchwood Boost, a program intended to create partnerships and spread the word about local nonprofits with missions tied to food. They also conduct food drives

Top left: Birchwood Café serves healthy food with a side of information on environmental issues. Photo by Kaie Cannon

Above left: The patio at Birchwood blooms in summer. Photo by Birchwood Café

Above right: Savory waffles arrive topped with healthy ingredients, mostly from local producers. Photo by Mette Nielson

and serve as a pickup location for seven community-supported agriculture programs that allow city residents to purchase fresh produce from regional farmers.

Open seven days a week, the Café has been enlarged from its original footprint, and you'll see friends and families with children lounging on the patio in summer. It's also a favorite with cyclists and runners who enjoy the nearby River Road and folks who make their way over from the nearby University of Minnesota.

3311 E. Twenty-Fifth St., Minneapolis
612.722.4474
birchwoodcafé.com

BREAKING BREAD CAFÉ

Here are all sorts of reasons to eat at Breaking Bread Café: job training for youth, supporting a fresh-food restaurant in a neighborhood of fast-food joints, community development . . . but, ultimately, you should go for the great food in a lively atmosphere with fun and friendly people.

Smiles from the staff and colorful artwork on the walls greet you when you enter Breaking Bread. Says Executive Chef Lachelle Cunningham, "On a typical day at the café, you will literally see people from every walk of life. Community members, community leaders, politicians, city workers, teachers, lawyers all come to break bread at this unique community hub, where the tables are set up family style to allow many opportunities to bump elbows with all kinds of people." Take a seat at the counter by the windows or at one of the long communal tables, and prepare to enjoy breakfast (served all day) or lunch until 3:00 p.m. The menu draws on the diverse culture of North Minneapolis for inspiration, and almost everything is made from scratch, including spice mixes, marinades, and sauces. For example, you can create your own biscuit sandwich, dive into gorgeous jerk shrimp and cheese grits, and munch a frittata or vegan quinoa cakes. The cafe features a list of daily specials, too, but whatever you do, be sure to order the coconut cornbread with orange-honey butter. You'll want to pack some into your cheeks to take home, like a chipmunk.

Lunch brings burgers and jerk shrimp po'boy sandwiches; chicken or vegan tacos; larger entrées, such as pot roast or dry rub chicken; and healthy salads, such as the citrus kale salad topped with orange slices, dried cranberries, sunflower seeds, and orange vinaigrette. For dessert, choose from homemade sweet-potato pie, peach cobbler, or cookies—all at prices that make Breaking Bread Café one of the better bargains in town. There's added value, according to Chef Lachelle, because "everything on the menu has an extra ingredient, love, that our customers can actually taste, and that is what I believe keeps them spreading the word and coming back again and again."

Behind the scenes, Breaking Bread is part of the organization

Top left: People from all around Minneapolis come for Breaking Bread's sunny atmosphere and friendly service.

Above left: Fabulous frittatas come with a side of coconut cornbread.

Above right: There's more than good food on the menu at Breaking Bread Café.

Appetite for Change, which supports an array of healthy food programs, including youth-led urban agriculture, industrial kitchen space for neighborhood food businesses, community cooking workshops, and more. In summer, the café features an outdoor patio. You can order food to go, and they cater too.

1210 W. Broadway Ave., Minneapolis
612-529-9346
breakingbreadfoods.com

BRIT'S PUB AND EATING ESTABLISHMENT

Anyone craving a bit of jolly old England will find it at Brit's Pub in the heart of downtown Minneapolis. Its motto is "serving scholars and scoundrels since 1990," but mostly you'll find nice people—and very few scoundrels—gathered in the wood-paneled tavern to enjoy a little camaraderie. They may be clinking glasses of imported British ale, European lager, or local brews. Others raise shots of the UK's famed whiskey. Brit's boasts a lengthy list—Highland, Lowland, Speyside, Islay, and some that hail from US distilleries too. Want to expand your Scotch horizons? Order a sampler.

But there's so much more going on at Brit's. Pair those beverages with munchies, such as mac and cheese bits, cod pieces, or scotch eggs. Blimey, Brit's serves up really good stick-to-your-ribs British fare, such as cornish pasties, fish and chips, bangers and mash, and shepherd's pie hearty enough to keep any shepherd full until the flock's in the barnyard. Lighter fare includes lovely salads and soups and an array of burgers and sandwiches. Main plates include Guinness pot roast and, from the days of colonial rule, Indian dishes such as chicken tikka masala. For dessert, Brit's serves sticky toffee bread pudding and the layered classic, trifle, with ginger sponge cake, mixed berry compote, mascarpone cream, and fresh lemon curd with crystallized ginger.

On any given night, you'll find Brits and non-Brits enjoying pub quizzes, scotch tastings, movie nights, and a live weekly podcast by the Crafty Rogues, a chap from Northern Ireland and a bloke from Australia. Not surprisingly, Brit's makes the perfect gathering place to watch football (that's soccer in American lingo) and rugby matches from around the world. While Brit's provides the perfect manly sort of atmosphere for sports viewing, it also serves a typical afternoon tea complete with dainty sandwiches, English cheeses, scones, and more, fit for the *Downton Abbey* set. It's also a favorite

Top right: On Brit's rooftop, lawn bowling and a view of downtown Minneapolis. Photo by Brit's Pub

Above left: Summer sidewalk dining in front of Brit's Pub. Photo by Brit's Pub

Above center: Traditional English trifle is among the desserts at Brit's Pub. Photo by Brit's Pub

Above right: Lawn bowling and a pint on Brit's Pub rooftop. Photo by Brit's Pub

spot for music lovers to grab dinner before or drinks after concerts at Orchestra Hall, directly across Nicollet Avenue from Brit's.

Probably the most notable feature at Brit's, however, is its 10,000-square-foot rooftop lawn bowling green, which offers both sport and a great view of downtown. Open only in warm weather, lawn bowling time is taken mostly by leagues and groups, but open bowling is available on Saturday and Sunday afternoons.

1110 Nicollet Mall, Minneapolis
612-332-3908
britspub.com

BRODERS' CUCINA ITALIANA, PASTA BAR, AND TERZO

A little bit of Italy resides at the intersection of Fiftieth Street and Penn Avenue in South Minneapolis, where the Broder family launched its Italian "deli," Cucina Italiana, more than thirty years ago. Which of these establishments to visit depends on your mood, as long as it's Italian food you seek.

The Cucina offers imported Italian deli meats, cheeses, pizza, stromboli, and luscious pastries. It's especially known for its handmade fresh pasta and sauces. You can order to go or eat in the Cucina's small dining area for a quick meal. It's also a foodie pleasure to peruse the shelves of Italian grocery products and household items.

With the Cucina's popularity, the family added the sit-down restaurant, the Pasta Bar, across the street. Broders' Pasta Bar capitalizes on the fresh pasta for which Broders' is famous. Along with such starters as roasted pancetta-wrapped pears or fried calamari and salads, you'll find a terrific offering of pasta dishes, including linguine

"South Minneapolis" (an amorphous descriptor encompassing the city's Southwest and Nokomis communities, and the Powderhorn community south of Lake Street) is characterized by quiet, tree-lined residential neighborhoods, abundant recreational spaces, and small, thriving local commercial districts. In recent years, South Minneapolis has also become a mecca for great chefs and their cozy, charming neighborhood eateries, including several James Beard Award-winning establishments and many more "Best of the Twin Cities" destinations in a variety of categories—all proof that great dining is an experience, not a destination.

Top right: Broders' Pasta Bar patio is a lovely stop on a summer evening to eat or to wait for a table inside. Photo by Kye Quirt

Top left: Broder's Cucina Italiana offers Italian specialty items and take-out food. Photo by Victoria Campbell

Above left: Terzo's Porchetteria is a walk-up window on the side of the building. It's open year-round and serves slow-roasted Italian pork sandwiches and bowls. Photo by Andy Swarbrick

Above right: Linguine con vongole at Broders' Pasta Bar features house-made egg pasta with button clams, red onion, pancetta, spicy peppers and white wine. Photo by Andy Swarbrick

with pan-seared branzino; fettuccine with shrimp, chickpeas, kale, dill, and feta, classics, such as fettuccine alla bolognese and house-made veal and pork cannelloni; and a list of wines from various regions of Italy. Beware of the wait for a table.

Terzo, Broders' newest restaurant, specializes in traditional Italian wines and a dinner menu that goes beyond the "primi" pasta course to offer "secondi" entrées of, for example, scallops, chicken involtini, glazed pork cheeks, and beef in Barolo sauce. Don't miss the Porchetteria at Terzo, a walk-up window open year-round, serving slow-roasted Italian pork sandwiches and bowls.

Cucina Italiana	Pasta Bar	Terzo
2308 W. Fiftieth St.	5000 Penn Ave. S.	2221 W. Fiftieth St.
Minneapolis	Minneapolis	Minneapolis
612-925-3113	612-925-9202	612-925-0330
broders.com/	broderspastabar.com	terzompls.com
cucina-italiana		

BRYANT-LAKE BOWL

What are you in the mood for—bowling, theater, music, comedy, film? You'll find just about anything that's up your alley, except automatic scoring, at this quirky, retro establishment. Here's some trivia: Bryant-Lake Bowl hosted the wrap party for Minnesota natives Joel and Ethan Coen's 1996 film *Fargo* and was a location for the movie *Beautiful Girls*. With all the fun things going on here near the corner of Bryant and Lake, it's easy to forget that it's a great food destination, too, and there's no need to lace up your bowling shoes to partake.

If microwave pizza and chicken fingers come to mind when you think "bowling alley food," you're in for a surprise. First of all, this Uptown institution opens at 8:00 a.m. daily, and that means breakfast. It offers dishes with organic eggs "plucked from the butts of Larry's chickens" in scrambles, rancheros, sandwiches, and omelets, to name a few, along with French toast, pancakes, oatmeal, and granola. The lunch and dinner menu features salads of greens, charred kale, or seared ahi tuna, all with house-made dressings. It also serves sandwiches and burgers—made with local, grass-fed beef, organic turkey, or black bean and sweet potato. Entrées run the gamut from pad thai and smoked Gouda pepper jack mac and cheese to fried chicken and biscuits, with changing meat and fish specials after 5:00 p.m. You'll find many of the same items on the late-night menu, so you can stoke up for more entertainment. Unlike

Just east of Lake Calhoun, Uptown is a Minneapolis commercial neighborhood that has long been a hub of entertainment and retail. It hosts a famous annual art fair and served as inspiration for the beloved Minnesota musician Prince's song "Uptown."

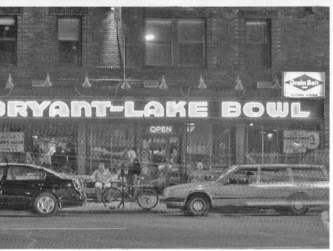

Top left: Bryant-Lake Bowl offers old-fashioned, low-tech bowling, entertainment, and great food. Photo by Bryant-Lake Bowl

Top right: Bryant-Lake Bowl is an Uptown, Minneapolis, institution. Photo by Bryant-Lake Bowl

Above left: Breakfast starts daily at 8:00 a.m. at Bryant-Lake Bowl. Photo by Bryant-Lake Bowl

Above right: No greasy bowling alley fare here. Instead, the menu offers luscious salads and other sophisticated casual fare. Photo by Bryant-Lake Bowl

your average bowling venue, Bryant-Lake Bowl serves cocktails and wine and sports one of the best beer selections around. Thrifty hipsters head for Cheap Date Night at Bryant-Lake Bowl, which offers two entrées, one bottle of wine or two pints of beer, and a round of bowling for a bargain price. Open daily from 8:00 a.m. to 2:00 a.m.

810 W. Lake St., Minneapolis
612-825-3737
bryantlakebowl.com

BUTCHER & THE BOAR

If you're a devotee of the three "B's" of American food and drink—beef, beer, and bourbon—welcome to Nirvana. A James Beard national award-nominated establishment and one of TripAdvisor's 25 Best Fine Dining Restaurants in the United States for 2015, Butcher & the Boar treats its guests to outstanding food and drink in a comfortable and fun atmosphere, accompanied by a hopping bar scene and one of the best beer gardens in the Twin Cities.

To be sure, Butcher & the Boar is a carnivore's delight. Beef and pork selections abound, including a menagerie of handcrafted sausages and grilled-to-perfection aged New York strips, prime rib, rib eyes, and double-cut pork chops. But alternatives to cow and pig also exist; fowl lovers can enjoy a wonderful pan-seared duck breast, and salmon, scallops, and daily seafood specials also grace the menu. A variety of ample, tasty appetizers, à la carte sides, and dessert offerings ensures that no one leaves Butcher & the Boar hungry.

Or, for that matter, thirsty. Butcher & the Boar offers more than twenty-five craft beers on tap, highlighted by numerous award-winning brews from the Twin Cities and beyond, plus a selection of imported bottled beers. Its extensive wine list is dominated by outstanding California reds and whites, with other top-notch Pacific Coast, French, and Italian wines on the card. It also features an assortment of classic and specialty cocktails.

But it's the bourbon card that merits special mention. On it you'll find six separate bourbon barrel selections, plus nearly a hundred separate bourbons and ryes from many of America's finest distilleries. If Canadian, Scotch, or Irish whiskeys are more to your liking, an ample supply of those is available too. If you can't decide on just one, bourbon and rye flights offer the opportunity to compare and savor different brands and styles.

Diners can choose from one of three dining-and-drinking options: the main restaurant and bar, festively serving the casual, the corporate, and everyone in between; an outdoor dining patio, also sporting the full menu; and a boisterous, year-round, dog-friendly covered beer garden, featuring sandwiches, sausages, bar snacks, beer, wine, and three dollar bourbon shots. Butcher & the Boar also

Top left: Butcher & the Boar has a popular beer garden, even in chilly weather. Photo by Sean O'Brien

Top right: Friends enjoy the beer garden with award-winning brews, wine, and cocktails too. Photo by Sean O'Brien

Above left: Butcher & the Boar's warm atmosphere makes a great date-night venue. Photo by Sean O'Brien

Above right: Searing ribs on the wood-fired grill. Photo by Sean O'Brien

offers two private dining rooms with prix fixe, chef-select menus for special events. Reservations for the restaurant and dining patio are recommended. The restaurant has a small parking lot adjacent to the building, and valet and off-street metered parking are also available.

1121 Hennepin Ave., Minneapolis
612-238-8888
butcherandtheboar.com

CAN CAN WONDERLAND

The adventure begins when you walk through the Invisible Secret Entrance. Go down some stairs, follow the arrows through a series of doors and hallways, and you'll arrive at your destination—Can Can Wonderland, a place that couldn't be more appropriately named. Inside this twenty-thousand-square-foot industrial space lies a wondrous combination of art, play, food, and entertainment designed to defy any categorization or convention.

Start with the name. Can Can Wonderland occupies what was the sprawling complex where the American Can Company once manufactured metal food cans for Carnation, Campbell's Soup, Del Monte, and many others. Can can, get it? The name is also an homage to the high-kicking, high-energy French music-hall dance of the 1800s. Makes total sense.

The central activity at Can Can is mini golf, with eighteen zany holes, each designed by local artists. Golfers must navigate a hallucinatory combination of fauna, flora, giant pink fuzzy creatures, water hazards, and even a hole evoking Grandma's living room. Vintage pinball machines (the kind from the '30s, '40s, and '50s) line the "Midway." Can Can's nightly stage shows may include an array of entertainment as varied and zany as you might expect here—big band, break dancing, ballet, amateur wrestling—a different experience every time.

Food at Can Can fits right into the carnival atmosphere. The Culinary Amusement Park features typical carnival food—hot dogs, nachos, and sweet and savory grilled sandwiches, ranging from grilled cheese to brisket to Spam. You'll find mini doughnuts with toppings, cotton candy, salads, and fruit and yogurt waffle cones.

Grab a cocktail at the Main Bar or the Wee Bar, both with a wild array of beverages. The list includes wine, Can Can canned beer, and a wondrous list of boozy adult floats, snow cones, and sodas. That Carrot Drink, for example, blends rum, sherry, carrots, edible "dirt" and is served in a flower pot. Even if it's not your birthday, try the HAPPY BIRTHDAY!!!!!! cocktail made from Bittercube Birthday Cake Vodka Blend, cream-cheese-frosting syrup, milk, sprinkles, sparklers, and poppers.

Top right: Can Can offers a crazy array of cocktails and adult floats.

Above left: Can Can Wonderland's super-secret entrance.

Above right: Carnival-style food ranges from cotton candy and milk shakes to hot dogs and grilled sandwiches.

On a serious note, Can Can Wonderland serves as an art-inspired engine of economic development in a formerly worn-down area. Now, it's a place you can bring your children, your rowdiest adult friends, grandparents, or hipsters. Don't try to understand it; just have fun.

755 Prior Ave. N., St. Paul
651-925-2261
cancanwonderland.com

CECIL'S DELI

Authentic Jewish delis are few and far between in the Twin Cities, but Cecil's is the real deal with food like your Bubbe makes. Enter through the deli section at Cecil's, where you'll find all sorts of meats, salads, and other kosher products. Pass through to the restaurant area filled with diners who represent just about every ethnicity in the Twin Cities happily enjoying the sort of food Cecil's has been serving since 1949.

Heart-warming chicken-noodle, chicken and matzo-ball soup and borscht top the menu, and the restaurant serves classic sandwiches with authentic lean corned beef, pastrami, chopped liver, and other meats layered between slices of fresh caraway rye, pumpernickel, black Russian rye, egg white, or whole-wheat bread. Sandwiches come in three sizes: regular (¼ pound), New York style (½ pound), and the giant Chazer piled with ¾ pound of meat. They arrive with homemade coleslaw or potato salad and a perfect kosher pickle.

Cecil's serves other hot and cold sandwiches, salads, desserts, and a selection of eggs, lox and bagels, and French toast for breakfast. The restaurant is open daily 9:00 a.m. to 8:00 p.m., the deli from 9:00 a.m. to 9:00 p.m.

651 S. Cleveland Ave., St. Paul
651-698-6276 (deli)
651-698-0334 (restaurant)
cecilsdeli.com

Top left: Cecil's is where Twin Citians go for authentic deli food.

Top right: Diners can order from Cecil's huge menu and dine in.

Above left: Sandwiches—corned beef, for example—come in three sizes: regular, New York style, and the hefty Chazer (¾ lb.).

Above right: Cecil's front-of-the-house deli offers all sorts of kosher foods.

CHEF SHACK RANCH

Standing inside Chef Shack Ranch—with its shabby-chic ranch house decor of rustic pressed tin walls, cow art, and kitschy knickknacks galore—you might expect to see a horse or a tractor parked outside. Instead, this is the place where Chef Shack's shiny red food trucks, some of the most popular around the Twin Cities, come to rest during the winter. It's also the brick-and-mortar locale where the award-winning chef/owners, Carrie Summer and Lisa Carlson, turn out casual, sophisticated food without pretense. The two have their roots in the fine dining world, but the casual menu at Chef Shack belies the complexity and precision with which the two create their food.

Each night you'll find a soup of the night (perhaps tomato-watermelon gazpacho), lovely salads, and burgers—bison or veggie. There's usually a taco of the night, tempeh reubens, and pulled pork or smoked brisket sandwiches. Sides include beans, biscuits, pickles, slaw, Thai hot wings, and whatever inspires the chefs, all made with fresh, organic ingredients. For dessert, be sure to order a pile of their trademark Indian-spiced mini doughnuts, nice and warm. The Shack features a short and interesting wine list and craft beers, which you can enjoy on its rustic patio in summer. There's also brunch on Saturday and Sunday. In addition, be sure to make a short road trip to the chefs' French eatery, also called Chef Shack, open weekends only in Bay City, Wisconsin.

3025 E. Franklin Ave., Minneapolis
612-354-2575
chefshackranch.com

Top: Chef Shack serves hearty yet complex food in a rustic farm atmosphere.

Above left: Brisket sandwiches are smoky perfection.

Above right: Mini doughnuts at Chef Shack have a hint of Indian spice.

CHIMBORAZO

In a metro area teeming with Asian, African, and Central American immigrants, this restaurant specializing in the South American cuisine of Ecuador stands out in more ways than one. Chimborazo—named after Ecuador's highest peak, a snow-capped volcano—has won accolades from diners and food critics alike as one of the Twin Cities' best ethnic eateries.

There's not much fancy or pretentious about Chimborazo. From the outside, it's a smallish, nondescript, stand-alone stucco building ensconced on the edge of a Nordeast residential area, across the street from a railroad yard. Its understated signage is easily missed by passing drivers, and the parking lot in the building's rear accommodates perhaps a dozen cars. Chimborazo's interior is equally basic but cozy, with fifteen to twenty tables nestled snugly among beautiful tapestries, great photographs of Ecuador, and a large blackboard listing the daily food and drink specials.

Ah, but then there's the food, which is nothing short of terrific. Specializing in traditional family fare from Ecuador and the Andean Highlands, it's easy to see why Chimborazo is such a favorite. Appetizers include fresh shrimp ceviche, cassava croquettes, llapingachos (traditional sweet-potato pancakes with cheese filling, fried egg, and peanut sauce), and fried green and sweet plantains. For entrées, diners may choose from a wonderful saltado (beef or vegetarian stir fry), hornado (roast pork with llapingachos), churrasco (grilled flank steak or chicken), chaulafan (Ecuadoran fried rice), encocado (fish or shrimp served in a coconut sauce), and many other indigenous dishes and daily specials. All entrées are accompanied by rice, plantains, or both, and salads and soups are available on the side. The tres leches dessert cake is to die for, and the drink card features a variety of excellent, reasonably priced South American wines, plus local beers. For the quality of its fare, Chimborazo is among the best dining values around; its ample entrées range from eleven to fifteen dollars, and all bottles of wine are half off on Wednesday date night.

Chimborazo opens for breakfast, lunch, and dinner seven days a week. It does not accept reservations, and during peak hours the line

Top left: Ecuadoran churrasco with grilled chicken.

Above left: Chimborazo's cooks turn out Ecuadoran specialties to please the line of hungry customers.

Above right: Chimborazo's saltado, a spicy stir fry of beef and vegetables.

often stretches into and through the narrow kitchen/serving area and up to (if not out) the back door. Happily, the queue generally moves fairly quickly. Free parking is available in the lot or on nearby streets.

2851 Central Ave. NE, Minneapolis
612 788-1328
chimborazorestaurant.com

CITY PARKS: GREAT EATS IN THE GREAT OUTDOORS

One of the greatest assets of the Twin Cities is the parks and lakes within their boundaries. Minneapolis, for example, has its famous Chain of Lakes that is part of the Grand Rounds National Scenic Byway. St. Paul has Como Regional Park, among others, and it contains the Como Zoo, Marjorie McNeely Conservatory, Como Lake, and much more. They make great places to bike, walk, boat, swim, listen to concerts—and eat! Below are some of the laid-back eateries in park pavilions, where you can combine fabulous outdoor recreation with the ultimate in al fresco dining in what are arguably the Cities' most scenic locales. The first three are seasonal restaurants, open only spring through fall. Check the websites for details. The last, Como Dockside, remains open year-round.

Set on the shore of Lake Calhoun, the Tin Fish is famous for fish tacos, fish sandwiches, and fish entrées that are fried or grilled. Yes, there are burgers and chicken, too, as well as ice cream, fountain drinks, beer, and wine.

Located in Minnehaha Park not far from the scenic Minnehaha Falls, Sea Salt specializes in seafood, such as shrimp, fish, and scallop tacos; oysters on the half shell; po' boy sandwiches; baskets with crab cakes or fried oysters. Beer and wine are also served. There's often music too.

Bread & Pickle is the Lake Harriet venue that serves just what you need for a meal in the park: hot and cold sandwiches, burgers, salads, and breakfast food that includes granola, organic scrambled eggs, and breakfast sandwiches with eggs or salmon—all with an emphasis on locally farmed ingredients. It also has ice cream cones and floats, and don't forget to buy a treat for your dog too. Stop in before or after a free concert in the Lake Harriet band shell.

Dockside is a year-round restaurant with a Creole/New Orleans focus. That means gumbo, po' boys, and such entrées as shrimp étouffée, and veggie options. Its full bar offers Southern classic cocktails as its signature drinks. Look for brunch on Saturday and Sunday, and check its calendar for musical events, trivia, movie nights, and more.

Left: Bread & Pickle serves food at Lake Harriet. Photo by Bob Rueckle

Right: Lakeside at Lake Harriet in Minneapolis. Select parks in Minneapolis and St. Paul offer free entertainment, great food, and an opportunity to enjoy the great outdoors. Photo by Bob Rueckle

The Tin Fish
3000 E. Calhoun Pkwy., Minneapolis
612-823-5840
tinfishmn.com

Sea Salt
4825 Minnehaha Ave., Minneapolis
612-721-8990
seasalteatery.wordpress.com

Bread & Pickle
4135 W. Lake Harriet Pkwy., Minneapolis
612-767-9009
breadandpickle.com

Como Dockside
1360 Lexington Pkwy. N., St. Paul
651-666-9491
comodockside.com

COOK ST. PAUL

Cook is the type of little neighborhood joint where you'd expect a warm greeting; simple, made-from-scratch, cozy food; and friendly service. Cook delivers all that but also beckons breakfast and lunch patrons to be adventurous with a hit of unexpected Korean flare that stimulates your palate and wakes up your mind. Fresh fruit receives a dash of lime juice, Korean chili flakes, and salt. There are plain breakfast pancakes or Korean pancakes—ground yellow beans mixed with spicy sausage, cabbage, and bean sprouts. Mac and Chi boosts the standard cheesy pasta with butter-fried kimchi, cream, and sharp cheddar served on cavatappi noodles. A favorite specialty: bibimbap. This rendering of a Korean favorite consists of a fried rice ball on a bed of chopped romaine hearts surrounded by Korean-flavored seasonal veggies, topped with a lightly poached egg—an awesome combination of sweet, sour, salty, smooth, and crispy.

Now that you're hooked, you'll want to visit Cook for its Friday night Korean Dinner, which sticks to straight-up Korean food. Says chef/owner Eddie Wu, "It is a hybrid of Korean street food, Korean bar food (called Anju), and traditional Korean dinner food, like the ribs."

As one diner commented, "Wu hoo!"

1124 Payne Ave., St. Paul
651-756-1787
cookstp.com

Top: Cook owner Eddie Wu likes to fuse Korean flavors with American favorites. Photo by Katie Cannon

Above left: The Trust Me, a sandwich with house-made peanut butter and kimchi. Photo by Bill Hickey

Above right: Bibimbap with pork belly.

COOKIE CART

Double chocolate chip, M&M, snickerdoodle, peanut butter, oatmeal raisin ... What's your favorite cookie? It's probably best to try them all at the Cookie Cart, just to be sure. Sit down in its cheerful and newly remodeled shop, have coffee, chat with the young people working behind the counter, or watch them baking through the window into the kitchen area. This is more than a big cookie shop. Cookie Cart provides teens fifteen to eighteen years old with job training, work, and life and leadership skills at this urban nonprofit bakery.

It started when Mercy Missionaries' Sister Jean Thuerauf recognized the need for meaningful, empowering work for young people in this neighborhood. She invited youth into her home for help with schoolwork and to learn to bake cookies. Word spread quickly, and the operation grew too large for her home. With community support, the business expanded to a pushcart that sold their cookies throughout north Minneapolis and eventually became a much larger operation in its current home. They'll box up a terrific selection of cookies for your next party, create a special gift box for your friend or sweetheart, and hand-decorate cookies for any event or holiday. They deliver too!

1119 W. Broadway Ave., Minneapolis
612-521-0855
cookiecart.org

Top right: Special gift boxes with cookies and other treats are available.

Above left: Trays of cookies tempt anyone with a sweet tooth.

Above center: Order cookies for events, or stop in for cookies and coffee.

Above right: The Cookie Cart is a professional cookie bakery with an additional focus on job training and life skills for local youth.

COOKS OF CROCUS HILL

If you're an ambitious home cook, if you want to be, or if you simply seek a culinary-related gift, Cooks of Crocus Hill has you covered. Their stores stock a fantastic and colorful array of pans, bakeware, knives, barware, coffeemakers, small kitchen appliances, every sort of cooking gadget, and cookbooks too.

Making paella? They'll sell you the special bomba paella rice from Spain to put in it and a big traditional pan to cook your ingredients, and they'll teach you how to make this Spanish favorite in a class in one of their beautiful teaching kitchens. At Cooks of Crocus Hill, they've turned cooking classes into social events. For example, check their calendar for regular "date night" cooking classes. They offer sessions for children and adults who want to learn the basics, who are looking for ideas for fast family meals, or who want to tackle more advanced ethnic and regional cuisine. The shops also serve as convenient places to pick up crop shares—portions of meat, poultry, and boxes of seasonal fruit and veggies, all raised on local farms. Look for Cooks of Crocus Hill's other locations in Edina and Stillwater and in several Kowalski's supermarkets in the metro area.

877 Grand Ave., St. Paul
651-228-1333
208 N. First St., Minneapolis
612-223-8167

cooksofcrocushill.com

Top right: Cooks of Crocus Hill carries specialized cookware and ingredients for just about any ethnic cuisine.

Above left: Paella class at Cooks of Crocus Hill.

Above right: Cooking appliances, towels, aprons, and unique ingredients for cooking or gifts.

COSSETTA ALIMENTARI

Founded in 1911 by an Italian immigrant as a tiny food market in St. Paul's "Little Italy," Cossetta is today a bustling, fourth-generation Italian deli, bakery, pastry shop, market, restaurant, and more, all under one enormous roof. Enjoy great pizza, pasta, and pastries, shop for hard-to-find Italian delicacies, sip a cup of espresso or a glass of prosecco, and experience firsthand the richness of St. Paul's ethnic heritage.

Any discussion of Cossetta necessarily begins with pizza. Made entirely from scratch, including house-kneaded dough, Cossetta's homemade tomato sauce, Italian sausage, and local mozzarella, Cossetta's pizzas are authentic, build-your-own Italian gems—crisp, chewy, delicious, and entirely without foofoo. Other items from Cossetta's counter-service eatery include yummy hot and cold Italian hoagies; lasagna and other pasta dishes; and classic chicken, veal, and

From the 1880s to the mid-1950s, the swampy mudflats of the Mississippi River below St. Paul's High Bridge were known as "Little Italy" because of the large number of Italian immigrants living there. Largely isolated from downtown St. Paul by geography and springtime floods, Little Italy developed into a self-sufficient community, albeit one surprisingly nonurban in character. In 1952, however, damage from a devastating flood caused St. Paul to pursue condemnation of the area, and by 1959 Little Italy ceased to exist. Today, Cossetta maintains a fascinating collection of historic photographs and other artifacts chronicling life in Little Italy during the first half of the twentieth century.

Top left: Imported Italian cheeses and meats at Cossetta.

Above left: Cossetta offers an incredible array of dining and shopping opportunities under one roof.

Above right: Italian pasta, sandwiches, pizza, and more may be ordered at the counter and eaten in the upstairs dining room.

sausage entrées. Diners seeking traditional Italian cuisine in a warm, comfortable, sit-down setting need only climb the stairs to Cossetta's own Louis Ristorante & Bar, featuring delectable antipasti, primi, secondi, contorni, and dolce selections, a terrific wine list, and a great rooftop view of St. Paul.

Seeking a romantic summer picnic? Pick up some of Cossetta's seventy-five to eighty house-made and imported salamis, prosciuttos, and other prepared meats, its sixty to seventy domestic and imported Italian cheeses, and a loaf of freshly baked Italian bastone from the bakery. Add a bottle of BYO wine and enjoy la dolce vita. Cossetta also features fresh steaks, chops, roasts, poultry, and produce; an enormous selection of imported pastas, sauces, and other Italian canned and dry goods; and a charming pasticceria teeming with mouthwatering cookies, cannoli, cakes, cream-filled concoctions, and mountains of gelato.

Cossetta accepts reservations for Louis Ristorante only. Complimentary parking can be found in Cossetta's attended adjacent lot, and valet service is also available.

211 Seventh St. W., St. Paul
651-222-3476
cossettas.com

COSTA BLANCA BISTRO

Costa Blanca, the fourth of Hector Ruiz's Latin-themed restaurants in Minneapolis, brings savory Mediterranean-themed tapas and a fun, stylish-yet-casual ambiance to the heart of Nordeast Minneapolis's eclectic dining scene. Ruiz spent his early years in the restaurant business in Mexico at the side of his mother; at Le Cordon Bleu, a Michelin three-star restaurant in Paris; and in the kitchens of several well-known Minneapolis eateries. Ruiz's abundant culinary experience shines at his other establishments—Café Ena (South American), La Fresca (nouveau Mexican), and Rincón 38 (tapas)— and at Costa Blanca his skills are revealed in delightful small plates that look as good as they taste.

Costa Blanca's menu is exclusively tapas, but if you think "tapas" is just some chichi name for "appetizers," think again. Costa Blanca's tapas are wonderfully creative, intricate, and flavorful works of art, gourmet mini entrées unto themselves. Consider, for instance, the pulpo, featuring braised octopus with roasted asparagus, artichokes, pimenton aioli, citrus aioli, spicy pimenton, sea salt, and microgreens. Or the piquillo peppers, stuffed with honey-truffle goat cheese and accompanied by sherry glaze, saffron aioli, red wine shallots, and microgreens. Even the jamón board features generous portions of serrano ham amidst manchego cheese, Basque olives, tangerine oil, garlic bread, and red-wine reduction.

With twenty-five to thirty beautifully prepared tapas on the menu nightly, Costa Blanca happily satisfies the solo diner looking for a quick bite and a glass of wine, lingering gatherings of friends looking to eat, drink, and talk the night away, and everyone in between. Seafood selections abound, including gambas (sautéed shrimp), conchas (seared scallops), pargo and cocochas (different preparations of red snapper), sea bass, calamari, octopus, and a creamy, tapas-sized seafood paella. Meat lovers will find the colitas (pimenton-marinated beef tips), lechon (pork tenderloin), lamb chops, and numerous ham and sausage offerings to their liking. And vegetarians need not fret; such plates as coliflor (pimenton fried cauliflower with fried olives and roasted artichokes), pipirana (vine-ripened tomatoes with red peppers and goat-cheese croquettes), and the aforementioned piquillo peppers will send them home delighted, as well.

Top left: Costa Blanca chef/owner Hector Ruiz has been cooking since he was a child in Mexico. Photo by Christy Neilson

Top right: Pulpo—charred risotto with pimenton, octopus, fried leeks, and saffron aioli. Photo by Christy Neilson

Above left: Gambas, shrimp in white wine butter sauce. Photo by Christy Neilson.

Above center: Perfect for vegetarians, piquillo peppers stuffed with truffle-honey goat cheese. Photo by Christy Neilson

Above right: At Costa Blanca, the beautiful dish Mero offers Chilean sea bass with truffle polenta, saffron butter sauce, and fennel slaw. Photo by Christy Neilson

Costa Blanca also features a yummy selection of Latin and American desserts; fine Spanish, Argentinian, and domestic wines by the bottle/glass; local craft beers; and classic and specialty cocktails. The restaurant is cozy, featuring both tables and bar seating, and reservations are highly recommended. On-street parking is available.

2416 Central Ave. NE, Minneapolis
612-789-9296
costablancabistro.com

DAKOTA JAZZ CLUB AND RESTAURANT

The Dakota, as they say, cooks. It's the Twin Cities' premier jazz venue and also brings a huge array of top national and international acts of other musical styles to its intimate space. Such stars as Prince, David Sanborn, Booker T. Jones, and the Preservation Hall Jazz Band have graced its stage. The music cooks, yes, but so does the Dakota's culinary talent. It's the rare music venue with a full-service menu on par with the entertainment. Simple snacks and cocktails are one option. The Dakota features a full bar with musically named cocktails—Amy Winehouse, Nina Simone, Raspberrry Beret Bellini, and more—as well as local brews and an extensive list of wine and scotch. Or go big with small plates that include mussels, kale salad, French onion soup, and steak tartare along with main courses such as chicken and sausage gumbo, trout, duck, pasta with scallops, and rotating specials. The Dakota sells prepaid premium dinner seating, which is closest to the stage. Regular seating is available, but reservations are highly recommended. Either way, it's okay and often encouraged to dance around your table.

Be sure to check out the Dakota's New Orleans-inspired sister jazz club, Vieux Carré, in St. Paul. It highlights a Creole-inspired menu, with music from Minnesota musicians.

1010 Nicollet Ave., Minneapolis
612-332-1010
dakotacooks.com

Top left: Flatbreads and spreads make great snacks while taking in a show at the Dakota. Photo by Shawn Neal.

Top right: Nightly jazz at the Dakota "cooks." Photo by Shellac Mueller

Above: Young hen with parmesan grits and grilled cipollini onion makes an elegant accompaniment to the music at the Dakota. Photo by Shawn Neal

DARI-ETTE DRIVE-IN

Each spring Dari-ette opens its windows and doors and lights up the big ice-cream cone sign in front. Workers uncover the outdoor menu boards and speakers at each parking space, where diners place orders to be delivered by carhops and eaten in the car (or at outdoor patio tables). Angela Fida represents the third generation of her family to carry out this ritual.

Built in 1951, Dari-ette sits next to what was originally the main road to Wisconsin. Few original 1950s drive-ins like this one are left, and you can bet that none of those offers great homemade Italian food. That might be what keeps families coming back decade after decade. They can order the typical drive-in fare—cooked-to-order burgers, hot dogs, fries, and chicken and shrimp dinners, along with ice-cream treats, milk shakes and '50s-style cherry or vanilla Coke. Yet, it's the spaghetti, antipasti salads, and homemade meatballs and sausage that set this tiny place apart, especially from chain drive-ins.

It's worth a trip to the easternmost reaches of St. Paul to experience this favorite, featured on *Diners, Drive-Ins and Dives* and other shows. So pile the family into the car and head east. While you're there, order Dari-ette's spaghetti sauce by the pint, quart, or gallon to take home.

1440 Minnehaha Ave. E., St. Paul
651-776-3470
No website but find them on Facebook

Dari-ette Drive-In is an original 1950s eatery where you can order and eat in your car.

EL BURRITO MERCADO

A family-owned-and-operated West Side St. Paul institution for nearly forty years, El Burrito Mercado is today a sprawling Mexican café, restaurant, bar, grocery, deli, bakery, and arts-and-crafts boutique, bringing an authentic "experiencia Mexicana" to Latinos and non-Latinos alike.

El Burrito Mercado features two year-round dining choices, a caféteria-style setting in the mercado itself and the La Placita bar/restaurant immediately adjacent to it. During warmer weather, outdoor dining and drinks on La Placita's spacious patio are also a popular option. All offer up an amazingly broad selection of authentic, classic Mexican favorites, including tasty burritos, enchiladas, tamales, and tacos stuffed with a dozen different pork, beef, chicken, shrimp, and veggie fillings, ranging in spiciness from Minnesota mild to Mexicali mouth-charring. Fajitas with a delicious mango-chipotle sauce, a terrific slow-cooked cochinito, and tender carne asada with onion and cactus are also among the house favorites. El Burrito Mercado serves breakfast, lunch, and dinner seven days a week, and reservations for La Placita are accepted.

El Burrito Mercado's grocery, one of the largest Hispanic groceries in the Cities, stocks hard-to-find specialty produce, meats, cheeses and other dairy products, and canned and packaged items. For serious cooks of authentic Mexican/Spanish cuisine, it's an essential stop. Gorgeous, colorful Mexican ceramics, metalworks, tapestries, and textiles, all handcrafted by Mexican artisans and all for sale, line the store's walls. El Burrito Mercado also offers live Latino entertainment on La Placita's patio and hosts celebrations of traditional Hispanic holidays and festivals, including one of the largest Cinco de Mayo fiestas in Minnesota.

175 Cesar Chavez St. #2, St. Paul
651-227-2192
elburritomercado.com

Left: Looking for salsa? You'll find every style.

Right: Classic Mexican dishes are served in both a casual café and in La Placita restaurant.

No community better reflects St. Paul's rich history of ethnic change than the West Side, located on and above low-lying flats adjoining the Mississippi River's southwest bank. Burdened by annual flooding, the West Side flats offered cheap housing for diverse waves of immigrants looking to create new lives for themselves in America—starving Irish Catholics in the 1850s and 1860s, Eastern European Jews fleeing religious persecution in the late 1800s, and Mexicans seeking work in area rail yards, factories, and stockyards after World War I. Along the way, each new group made the area its own; for example, Torre de San Miguel, now a Latino landmark, is actually the surviving bell tower from an Irish Catholic church built in 1867. Today, the West Side is largely Hispanic, home to many of the thirty thousand Latinos—10 percent of the city's population—who call St. Paul home.

ESKER GROVE

Artful cuisine set amidst modern art. That's the experience at Esker Grove, a 2017 James Beard semifinalist for Best New Restaurant in the US. Esker Grove has risen to the unusual challenge of creating a food and dining experience that matches its setting inside the Walker Art Center, one of the five most-visited museums of modern art in the US.

Not surprisingly, the dishes that arrive are arranged on the plate with artfulness that matches the environment. They're so beautiful on the plate that you may want to take them home and hang them on the wall rather than eat them . . . but that would be a mistake. Admire your meal for a minute, post a few pics to Instagram, and then dig in.

You might expect weird food in this avant-garde atmosphere, perhaps more pretentious than tasty. Yet, Esker Grove didn't earn its reputation with uber gourmet combinations or with tiny bits of unrecognizable food set on the plate with tweezers. Instead, at its core, Esker Grove is all about great cooking, with fresh ingredients prepared with attention to detail and a lot of thought about the dining experience it wants to create—as they say, "a layered sensory experience of food: taste, visual, texture, aroma." The lunch menu offers simple plates: for example, avocado toast, a plate of charcuterie to nibble, gorgeous salads, and larger dishes, such as gnocchi with lamb ragout and fennel. At dinner, you'll find a changing array of starters, such as a celery root tart; vegetarian main dishes such as cauliflower with preserved mushrooms, onion, and puffed wild rice; and other entrées, such as roasted sturgeon, capon, lamb shoulder, and, yes, even a steak. Save room for budino, a dessert that blends the flavors of butterscotch, chocolate, almond, pretzels, and malted ice cream. You can also pop in simply for a cocktail and bar snacks, such as eggplant tartine or fried chicken sliders served with mole sauce, avocado, and cilantro.

These dining options are meant to combine perfectly with a tour of the Walker's galleries, exhibitions, and events. In fact, Esker Grove's space flows seamlessly into the Walker's world of art. You'll dine next to a floor-to-ceiling collage by local artist Frank Big Bear titled *Universes Collide*. Only a glass wall separates Esker Grove from the

Top: The colorful Esker Grove salad with herbs, seaweed, and vegetables.

Above left: Eating at the Walker Art Center's Esker Grove means dining with art.

Above right: Food is flavorful and appropriately artistic.

museum's lobby on one side, and on the other side a wall of windows looks out onto its famed Sculpture Garden and downtown.

Esker Grove doubles in size when its huge terrace opens in warm weather. Arty black apparel optional.

723 Vineland Place, Minneapolis

612-375-7542

eskergrove.com

FARMERS' MARKETS

People in the Twin Cities love their farmers' markets. In fact, more than fifty can be found in the metro area, with many small neighborhood markets in Minneapolis, St. Paul, and surrounding suburbs. They're generally open from April through fall, with special open times and venues during the winter and holidays. All offer a colorful array of the fruits and veggies that we wait for all winter, along with locally made cheeses, meats, artisan goods, garden plants, and cut flowers. The three listed below are the biggest markets. Each has its own character and offers its own tasty slice of Twin Cities culture. Tour these markets and you'll meet some of the people who bring their distinctive food and culture to the Twin Cities and contribute to the vibrant culinary scene.

The Mill City Farmers' Market in Minneapolis is situated between historic flour mills, the Guthrie Theater, and the Mississippi River, with much of the market housed under the old railroad shed where trains brought grain to the mill. It features more than 125 vendors, including farmers, bakers, artisans, and those offering ready-to-eat food. Produce comes primarily from local organic farms and from urban farms in Minneapolis and St. Paul. Market goers may take their purchases and eat by the Mississippi River, with the Pillsbury A-Mill in the distance. Or they can sit on the steps adjacent to the Guthrie Theater.

The Minneapolis' Farmers' Market is the larger of the two major Minneapolis markets, with a satellite market downtown on Thursdays in summer (check the website for Thursday locations). It's a huge market and offers both locally grown produce and some trucked in from warmer climes. You'll find a large assortment of garden plants, funky arts and crafts, and purveyors of all sorts of meat, cheese, breads, specialty sauces, and condiments. Satisfy the appetite you've worked up shopping with grilled brats, corn, tacos, and more to eat at the market.

A tradition since the 1850s, the St. Paul Farmers' Market resides in the historic Lowertown neighborhood. Vendors here are required to sell local produce grown within fifty miles of the market,

Left: Farmers' market tomatoes of every stripe and color.

Right: The folks from Real Foods Farm bring their organic produce to the Mill City Farmers' Market.

guaranteeing super fresh fare. It's a foodie destination with not only produce but also bakery goods, cheese, poultry, buffalo, venison, beef, pork, lamb, maple syrup, eggs, flowers, plants, shrubs, and many other items.

Mill City Farmers' Market
704 S. Second St., Minneapolis
612-341-7580
millcityfarmersmarket.org

Minneapolis Farmers' Market
312 E. Lyndale Ave. N., Minneapolis
612-333-1737
mplsfarmersmarket.com

St. Paul Farmers' Market
290 E. Fifth St., Saint Paul
651 227 8101
stpaulfarmersmarket.com

FASIKA

For a first-timer, stepping into Fasika feels like a tiny trip to Ethiopia, though you've only traveled as far as this unassuming little place on St. Paul's Snelling Avenue. The alluring scent of exotic spices signals unexplored territory. Yet, if the number of people lined up to wait for a table are any clue, you're on safe ground.

"Fasika" is the Ethiopian word for Easter, connoting happiness and celebration. Here it also translates to a festive, communal dining experience. If your mother told you to mind your manners and hold your utensils properly at the dinner table, you'll love Fasika, where eating with your fingers is the order of the day. Instead of using silverware, you get to sop up the food and sauces with the Ethiopian bread, injera, which is like a giant spongy pancake. Injera is commonly made with teff, a nutritious Ethiopian staple grain, sometimes mixed with wheat flour. Order one (or more) of the beautiful sampler platters so that everyone in your group can dig into the huge shared dishes and taste each item. Your server will bring silverware if you ask, and you can eat from your own plate, but entering into the communal spirit and eating from shared platters is more fun.

Luckily, the menu explains each of the dishes, which feature beef, lamb, chicken, fish, and a great selection for vegetarians that includes greens, lentils, split peas, and vegetable curries. Ethiopia's location on the Horn of Africa has made it part of the spice trade for millennia, so expect plenty of flavor. You'll find two key spice combinations. One is berbere, a blend of chili peppers, garlic, onion, and other spices that yields a flavorful and warm sauce. The other is mitmita, a similar though hotter spice combination. Some versions include cardamom, cloves, and sometimes cinnamon, cumin, and ginger. Fasika offers a selection of wine and domestic beer and several tasty Ethiopian beers, as well. Because Ethiopia is the original home of the coffee arabica plant, you may prefer to choose a cup of strong Ethiopian coffee. While you're eating, be sure to pay attention to the soft East African music in the background that occasionally includes unique covers of Bee Gees and Taylor Swift tunes and other pop music. Fasika is open daily, 11:00 a.m. to midnight.

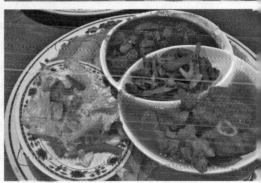

Top right: Veggie heaven is a Vege Sampler with seven dishes, such as curried vegetable stew, Ethiopian-style greens, curried split peas, lentils in berbere sauce, and more.

Above left: Fasika serves a variety of Ethiopian beers, including this amber style.

Above center: Embroidered curtains at Fasika.

Above right: A lamb sampler, (enough for two) includes curried lamb stew, lamb stew with berbere sauce, and marinated lamb with peppers onions, garlic, and rosemary.

510 Snelling Ave. N., St. Paul
651-646-4747
fasika.com

FIKA

In Sweden, fika is a daily break, like a coffee break. In Minneapolis, Fika is the "New Nordic"-inspired café at the American Swedish Institute and offers much more than coffee or standard museum café fare. It's widely recognized as one of the best places to have lunch in the Twin Cities.

Even on the grayest of winter days, Fika shines with a bright and airy atmosphere, complete with spare contemporary Scandinavian design, huge windows, and a crowd of fair-haired folks decked out in fancy Nordic sweaters. Many arrive to tour the thirty-three fascinating and ornate rooms of the Institute's historic Turnblad Mansion, to view the rotating exhibitions of Scandinavian art, or to participate in cultural events that include music, film, and crafts. It's no surprise, though, that many people come just for the food.

Fare at Fika follows the movement that elevated Nordic cuisine to haute cuisine by using traditional ingredients in new ways—no lutefisk in sight (see Ingebretsen's, page 80). Here they serve some of the best meatballs you'll ever eat, a far cry from the bland beige orbs you've probably tasted at a party buffet. Fika's juniper-spiced meatballs (ordered at the counter and delivered to your table) arrive on small plates with potato purée, cucumber, lingonberry, and mustard sauce. Delish, or, as the Swedes might say, "utsökt."

The menu includes smorgasar, open-faced sandwiches topped with, for example, lamb shoulder, lemon yogurt, cucumbers, and dill on caraway rye bread. Or, try the gravlax—house-cured salmon with deviled egg, onion jam, and capers on Danish rye. Every dish is as colorful and appealing to the eye as it is to the palate. Follow your meal with a little cardamom bread pudding for dessert. Fika also offers a nice selection of beer, wine, and specialty cocktails, along with coffee and house-made sodas.

Used as a verb, to fika means to set aside a moment for quality time. Fika is a great place to do that for breakfast and lunch daily (except Monday) and for happy hour and dinner on Wednesday evenings. In summer, guests enjoy outdoor dining in the Institute's beautiful courtyard, which is like dining next to a fairy-tale castle. Be sure to stop in the terrific Scandinavian gift shop for a souvenir.

Top left: Fika is located in the American Swedish Institute. Photo by Jon Dahlin

Top right: The scene at Fika is colorful, contemporary, and packed with lunchtime diners. Order at the counter and servers deliver the food to your table. Photo by Jon Dahlin

Above left: These aren't your grandma's Swedish meatballs. Photo by Jon Dahlin

Above right: This open-faced sandwich includes pork and smoked trout sausage, asparagus, fennel, sea bean, citrus crème fraiche, and pine nuts on caraway rye bread. Photo by Jon Dahlin

American Swedish Institute (asimn.org)
2600 Park Ave., Minneapolis
612-871-4907
fikaCafé.net

FOOD TRUCKS

Ah, there's just something about hitting the road. Every spring a fleet of itinerant food trucks bursts forth from its winter rest, cruising the Twin Cities to satisfy citizens who've been waiting all winter for the unique eats they serve. Many trucks hibernate during the winter, but others operate year-round catering food at special events or cheerfully filling the tummies of patrons outside local brewery tap rooms. Many well-known Twin Cities restaurants have refined their fare and tested culinary concepts with these four-wheeled restaurants—Chef Shack, Hola Arepa, and World Street Kitchen, to name just a few. Conversely, such restaurants as Market Bar-B-Que that have long experience in real buildings now get in gear by making their eats available from food trucks, too.

They're an elusive bunch, and it's often hard to pin down their locations. You'll see them in downtown Minneapolis and St. Paul on weekdays, parked near some of the Cities' largest office buildings. They regularly set up at farmers' markets and summer music and arts festivals. Some festivals, such as the Uptown Food Truck Festival, take place especially to celebrate these rovers. Once you get to know your favorites, the best way to keep tabs on trucks is to follow them on brewery calendars or on Twitter, where they tweet their current locations. If you're new to the Twin Cities food truck scene, here are a few standouts to get you started:

O'Cheeze (crazy-good variations of grilled-cheese sandwiches)
@O_Cheeze

Curious Goat (goat burritos, burgers, and more)
@CuriousGoatMN

Market Bar-B-Que (barbecued classics)
@MarketBBQ

Wyn65 (fried chicken and more)
@Wyn_65

The Cave Café (Afro-Italian fusion)
@TheCaveCafé

Left: Chef Shack began as a food truck and operates at a stationary location, Chef Shack Ranch, too.

Right: Hola Arepa food trucks sell Venezuelan street food.

Midnord Empanada Truck (Spanish empanadas, Minnesota style)
@MidNordTrucks

The Moral Omnivore (organic eclectic)
@Moral_Omnivore

Potter's Pasties (traditional savory pasties and pies)
@PottersPasties

Tot Boss (creative tater tot concoctions)
@TOTBOSStruck

Gastrotruck
@Gastrotruck

Café Racer (Latin American street food)
@Caféracermn

Tatanka Truck (Native American)
@TatankaTruck

Kabomelette (kabobs and omelets)
@kabomelette

FOREPAUGH'S RESTAURANT

Looking for Victorian elegance in a lovingly restored nineteenth century mansion? Check. Fine classic dining? Absolutely. Comfy bistro/bar and rooftop deck with a view? Got 'em both. Chef's table set within a gorgeous, cozy wine cellar? Ditto. Resident ghosts? Yep, that too—or so they say. Welcome to Forepaugh's, where generations of St. Paulites have celebrated birthdays, anniversaries, weddings, graduations, and holidays; savored a great meal; or simply kicked back after a hard day in the office.

Built in 1870, this Victorian mansion was originally the family home of Joseph Forepaugh, a wealthy dry goods merchant. After Forepaugh sold it in 1886, the mansion changed ownership many times and was later converted into a boarding house. In 1976, after years of renovation, the mansion opened as a restaurant and today is fully restored to its former Victorian grandeur.

On its second and third floors, Forepaugh's offers elegant dinner fare, including steaks, chops, beef Wellington, and pan-seared walleye, accompanied by a variety of savory first and second courses. The first floor features a wonderful Victorian bar and parlor with Forepaugh's "downstairs" menu, made up of delicious burgers, classic sandwiches, mac-and-cheese, a scrumptious poutine, and other pub treats. A delightful rooftop deck overlooking Irvine Park is a favorite on summer evenings, and a well-stocked, limestone-walled wine cellar and chef's table present an unforgettable fine dining atmosphere.

And then there are the ghosts. As legend has it, Joseph Forepaugh and one of his housemaids, a colleen named Molly, were having an adulterous affair before Forepaugh committed suicide in 1892, whereupon Molly purportedly hanged herself from a third-floor chandelier in the family's new Summit Avenue home. Although neither of them met their demise at the old Exchange Street mansion, restaurant staff and patrons alike have reported numerous ghostly Joseph and Molly sightings over the years, especially at weddings—perhaps envious of the happy (living) couple's new life together.

For insatiable Victorian era fans, consider dining at Forepaugh's after a tour of the Alexander Ramsey House, the mansion-turned-

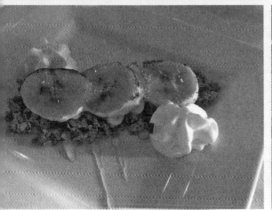

Top left: Forepaugh's occupies an elegant Victorian mansion, perhaps with a resident ghost.

Top right: A brunch omelet with peppers, green onions, and gruyere.

Above left: Desserts may include this "deconstructed" banana cream pie with bananas and crunchy pralines.

Above right: Forepaugh's has seating on several levels, including this special dining room in the wine cellar.

museum of Minnesota's first territorial governor directly across the street; alternatively, stop in for food and drink before a Minnesota Wild game at nearby Xcel Center. Forepaugh's accepts reservations and is open for happy hour and dinner nightly (except Mondays) and for Sunday brunch. Ample free parking exists across the street from the restaurant, and valet service is also available.

276 S. Exchange St., St. Paul
651-224-5606
forepaughs.com

GANDHI MAHAL

Curry, cumin, turmeric . . . the fragrant scent of Indian spices greets diners at the door of Gandhi Mahal, and even before you settle into your seat, this gracious eatery's jewel-like colors set a mood that suggests you're about to experience Indian food with something extra. Here they strive to pique your taste buds with food cooked in the style of Bangladesh and northern India, using family recipes and produce from their own gardens and local farmers' markets when possible. Appetizers include vegetable-filled samosas served with tamarind, onion, and green chutney; and onion bujia, fritters with onions, veggies, and lentils. The lengthy list of entrées, or rosai, features traditional tandoori dishes cooked in clay pots and specialties such as Delhi tikka masala (with tomato cream and fenugreek) and tilapia cooked with Bangladeshi spices. Diners may order most dishes with tofu, vegetables, beef, lamb, chicken, fish, or shrimp and specify the preferred spice level, mild to extra hot. Many menu items appear on the sizable lunch buffet.

While turning out palate-pleasing food, the folks at Gandhi Mahal also seek to inspire others with their ethos of harmony with people and the environment. There's an aquaponics system in the basement and honeybees on the roof. Don't miss the graphic on the front window that illustrates the owner's journey from Bangladesh to Minnesota and the Gandhi quote, "Be the change you want to see in the world."

3009 Twenty-Seventh Ave. S., Minneapolis
612-729-5222
gandhimahal.com

Top right: A window mural traces the owner's path from Bangladesh to Minnesota.

Above left: Gandhi Mahal serves food in a colorful setting.

Above right: Striving for fresh food and environmental harmony, Gandhi Mahal sources much food here from local gardens and farmers' markets.

GASTHOF ZUR GEMÜTLICHKEIT

Looking for perpetual Oktoberfest? You'll find it at Gasthof zur Gemütlichkeit (GzG), a rollicking Tyrolean-style lodge famous locally for its tasty German food and beer, lusty sing-alongs, lederhosen- and dirndl-clad servers, and raucous celebration of all things Bavarian.

Any description of GzG begins with beer. GzG features big-brewery German beers on tap, including Paulaner, Warsteiner, Hacker-Pschorr, and König Ludwig; these come in half- and full-liter steins and "Das Boot," a two-liter glass boot recommended, thankfully, for sharing. Also on tap are twenty to twenty-five domestic beers and ciders, and many more in bottles and cans. For non-beer-drinking heretics, GzG offers red, white, and sparkling wines, a full bar, and specialty cocktails. But beer drinkers rule, and bar and dining room alike regularly echo with full-throated chants of "Ein prosit!" and "Zicke zacke, zicke zacke. Hoi! Hoi! Hoi!" as birthdays, anniversaries, and other special events—real or feigned— are toasted by all.

For the hungry, GzG offers a full menu of delicious German dishes, including wienerschnitzel (breaded veal cutlet), sauerbraten (beef roast), käseschnitzel (breaded pork cutlet with cheese sauce), hühnchen (breaded chicken breast in peppercorn sauce), kasseler rippchen (smoked pork chops), and, of course, GzG's grilled meter-long bratwurst, accompanied by a small mountain of sauerkraut. Spätzle and red cabbage accompany most entrées, and dessert specialties include authentic apple strudel and Black Forest torte. GzG also features combination platters, which, though labeled as "for two," could nourish a small Bavarian village. Steak and seafood entrées fill out the menu.

No proper Bierstube lacks live oompah music, and GzG delivers here, as well. On the main level, wandering Tyrolean-attired accordionists squeeze out everything from German folk ballads and beerhall tunes to Elvis hits and PG-rated drinking songs. Singing is all but mandatory; vocal training is not. On Saturday nights, GzG's

Top right: "Bayrische Hausplatte," or Bavarian House Platter, offers a sample of Bavarian specialties, such as rouladen, smoked pork chops, and house-made German sausage.

Above left: German beers on tap come in half- and full-liter steins.

Above right: German specialties, such as spaetzle with pork loin and red cabbage, are typical Gasthof fare.

lower-level Keller Bar features a live polka band, ample dance floor, picnic-table seating, and plenty of beer and bar snacks. During Oktoberfest proper, GzG's parking lot becomes a sprawling tented beer garden with live music, thousands of beer-loving customers, and some of the best fun in the Cities.

GzG accepts reservations for dining room tables. The Keller Bar and main floor bar are extremely popular with college students and twenty- and thirty-somethings, especially on weekend nights, and become crowded early. Parking is available in GzG's adjoining parking lot and on area streets.

2300 University Ave. NE, Minneapolis
612-781-3860
gasthofzg.com

GLAM DOLL DONUTS

Glam Doll, you're so hard to resist. Your doughnuts are visually stunning, artful "cake-raised-filled-fritter-tastic goodness," served up with a touch of pinup girl glamour and pink tutu flair.

Head inside Glam Doll's sassy retro storefront to peruse the cases full of provocatively named doughnuts, such as Daddy Dearest with Surly beer icing and bacon crumb topping; the Varga Girl with almond cream, chocolate, and shaved almonds; or the savory doughnuts, such as the Girl Next Door with havarti and muenster filling and beer glaze with bacon crumbs. Order doughnuts one at a time, and hang out to eat them with coffee in the colorful back room that features a rotating collection of works by area artists. Or fill a pink boxful. Glam Doll's second location in Northeast Minneapolis has a larger menu that features beer and doughnut pairings. Some doughnuts here are a meal in themselves: for example, the Belly Bomb, a mac and cheese creation that comes with vegetarian chili. The Countess combines turkey and American cheese on a glazed doughnut covered in powdered sugar and served with a side of fresh strawberry jam. The Old School Rose doughnut is a glazed doughnut with mozzarella cheese, marinara sauce, and pepperoni inside. Both locations are open until 1:00 a.m. Friday and Saturday nights.

2605 Nicollet Ave. S., Minneapolis
612-345-7064

519 Central Ave. NE, Minneapolis
612-223-8071

glamdolldonuts.com

Top: Glam Doll's sassy exterior.

Above left: Order from the list of sugary confections, and stay for coffee.

Above right: You'll find an amazing variety of doughnuts, crullers, and fritters, including the Scream Queen with chocolate and bacon.

GYST FERMENTATION BAR

If you like your food colorful, creative, and with a pinch of pucker, Gyst is the place for you. "Gyst" derives from an old English word for yeast, which is one of the primary components of the fermentation process used to make, for example, beer, cheese, or sourdough bread.

While people have been fermenting their food since, well, since there have been people, fermented food has gained new attention for its health benefits and distinctive flavors. Many great foods that you may not have known are fermented, for example, meats, such as salami, are both cured and fermented to add flavor and control moisture. Did you know that fermentation of cocoa beans allows the flavor of chocolate to develop? That's the "gist" of the story at Gyst, where the menu centers on fermented food and beverage pairings that "create unusual and diverse flavors and flavor combinations."

Owners Mel and Ky Guse are sisters who grew up in South Dakota. As grown-ups, they lived in San Francisco but later returned to the Midwest to be closer to family. Their establishment has a hip, "neighborhoody" vibe, where you feel welcome no matter where you live. Settle in at a table or perch at the bar and chat with the staff, who are happy to explain the Gyst concept, where the food comes from, and how it's made. As one server put it, "We're geeky about fermentation."

Go with a plan to taste lots of things. The "Motherboard" provides that opportunity with an artful combination of salumi, cheese, and pickled veggies to explore and savor. Be open to unexpected flavor combinations, such as the "Sandor," an open-faced kimchi and peanut butter sandwich. Gyst serves the best pickled eggs ever, pickled in beet juice so they're pretty as well as yummy. You can purchase many of the in-house-fermented pickles and artisanal cheeses so that you can add interest and pucker to your meals at home.

The menu also includes drinks, such as kombucha, cider, fermented teas, and beer. The wine list offers naturally fermented wines that you won't find many other places.

Don't bother to leave a tip. At Gyst, they believe food workers

Top left: The "Motherboard" features a gorgeous assortment of cheese, meats, pickled vegetables, and more—great for sharing. Photo by Tommy Nolan

Top right: The wine list features spontaneously fermented wines. Photo by Tommy Nolan

Above left: Grilled cheese with sauerkraut on a baguette. Photo by Tommy Nolan

Above right: Sisters Ky and Mel Guse at their restaurant, Gyst. Photo by Jackie Adelman

should be treated as skilled professionals and earn a living wage. Consequently, prices on the menu reflect the 15 to 20 percent extra you may have left as a gratuity.

Stop in before or after a visit to the nearby Minneapolis Institute of Art (at 2400 Third Avenue South). You'll feel thoroughly cultured in more ways than one.

25 E. Twenty-Sixth St., Minneapolis
612-758-0113
gystmpls.com

HANDSOME HOG

Teetotalling vegetarians, please feel free to turn the page now. Nothing to see here, so keep on moving, but if you're not, welcome to hog heaven. A delightful blend of contemporary Southern cuisine, carnivorous pleasures, and one of the most extensive bourbon collections in the Twin Cities, Handsome Hog brings the New South to St. Paul's Lowertown Historic District with style and verve.

Let's start with the food. The menu centers on traditional Southern treats, including shrimp and grits, sausage gravy poutine, hush puppies, gumbo, barbecue, chicken fried steak, ribs, beef brisket, collard greens, and what might be the best buttermilk biscuit with smoked honey butter on the planet. Make no mistake, pork is king here, but contemporary touches abound. The brisket sandwich, for instance, is topped with pickled watermelon rind, adding unexpected sweetness and flavor to the meat, while chunks of smoked pork and a tangy vinegar sauce inhabit the collard greens. The terrific "Meat Bar" serves up one of the best charcuterie plates around, with generous samplings of house-cured and Red Table-procured smoked pork products surrounded by vegetables pickled right downstairs in the basement, sun-dried grape tomatoes, and a variety of homemade mustards, all wonderfully and artistically arranged on the serving platter. One almost—almost—hates to disturb its beauty.

The libations are equally impressive. Handsome Hog's "Brown Bible" features more than a hundred different bourbons, ryes, and American, Canadian, Irish, and Scotch whiskies, plus a variety of classic and signature cocktails, most bourbon-based. Looking for some twenty-three-year-old Pappy Van Winkle to impress your client and deplete your expense account? You'll find it here. Handsome Hog also offers a nice selection of local craft beers on tap, plus domestic and imported cans and bottles, and wines by the glass. And no Southern restaurant would be complete without sweet tea, which Handsome Hog brews by the barrelfull.

Not to be overlooked are Handsome Hog's architecture and location. The restaurant is situated in the historic Noyes Bros. & Cutler building, constructed in 1886 and now known as Park Square Court. It overlooks Mears Park, home to weekly summer concerts and other outdoor special events. The Green Lantern, a downstairs

Left: A charcuterie plate from Handsome Hog's Meat Bar.

Right: Handsome Hog resides in a historic building in St. Paul's Lowertown neighborhood.

speakeasy and music venue, adjoins Handsome Hog and provides a convenient and cozy landing place for post-pork celebrating.

Handsome Hog does not accept reservations, and diners are seated on a first-come, first-served basis. Valet parking is available, and garage and on-street parking are also nearby.

203 E. Sixth St., St. Paul
651-340-7710
handsomehog.com

HI-LO DINER

From the outside, it looks like a meal at the Hi-Lo Diner could be a kitschy trip back to the 1950s. Yes, this vintage 1957 diner was split in two and trucked in from a town near Pittsburgh, and its new owners restored and buffed its classic lines to a gleaming shine and crowned it with a funky neon sign.

In short order, you'll find this diner's atmosphere and menu is of a more contemporary style. It's a hipster haven and a family/neighborhood place, too, with cheery turquoise booths and a patio in summer. It's no greasy spoon either. With a made-from-scratch menu, the basic diner fare here is so good that it could be considered *haute diner*. As one man sitting at the counter offered, "Have you been here before? Everything here is awesome."

You can order breakfast all day at Hi-Lo. For lunch and dinner, try sandwiches, such as the pastrami silo, and standards such as meatloaf that incorporates thyme, onion, garlic, and dried cherries. Hi-Lo's signature dish: the High Top, a square doughnut, not too sweet, that comes with sweet or savory toppings and fillings. For example, the Gary Cooper comes with buttermilk fried chicken, maple-bourbon syrup, country gravy, and micro arugula. Or the Po'Boy Dough Boy arrives with Argentinian shrimp, adobo slaw, and a cilantro lime aioli. The Quack of Dawn High-Top is topped with duck confit, a poached egg, hollandaise, crispy shallots, tarragon, and griotte cherries. Sweet High Tops, such as the Minneapolis Bliss, feature baked apples, sea-salt caramel, créme fraiche, and candied pecans.

While you're stuffing in all these goodies, don't forget that the Hi-Lo has a rotating list of gorgeous pies that may include the classic lemon meringue, french silk, black bottom banana cream, or Walt Whipman, which layers a sugar cookie crust with malted milk-chocolate ganache, crushed malted milk balls and crisp and caramelized pastry flakes, topped with whipped cream and malted milk balls. Too full already? They're available for purchase to take home.

The atmosphere becomes even livelier at Hi-Lo in the evening. This diner has a full bar serving craft cocktails, local brews, adult shakes and floats, and ice-cream cocktails.

Open daily (except Monday). Check the schedule for afternoon and late-night happy hours.

Top left: Traditional diner food with a colorful and spicy spin. Photo by Eliesa Johnson Photography

Top right: Sit at the counter, or tuck into a booth. Photo by Eliesa Johnson Photography

Above left: The Hi-Lo Diner is a shiny vintage diner from 1957. Photo by Eliesa Johnson Photography

Above right: Hi-Lo serves craft cocktails, local brews, and adult ice-cream drinks. Photo by Eliesa Johnson Photography

4020 E. Lake St., Minneapolis
612-353-6568
hi-lo-diner.com

HOLA AREPA

Say hello to Hola Arepa, a lively eatery that buzzes with a sunny South American vibe, even in Minnesota's coldest winter months. The business started as a food truck that became a favorite among the downtown lunch crowd and introduced Latin street food to the streets of Minneapolis. It also introduced its namesake dish, arepas, which are small pancake-like disks made from cornmeal dough that's flattened into patties and cooked to crispy perfection on a griddle. Arepas arrive topped or stuffed with meats, veggies, cheese, and homemade aioli or chimichurri sauce. The food truck's success drove its owners to open a brick-and-mortar Hola Arepa in what was formerly a 7-Eleven. *Food and Wine* magazine soon featured the new venue on its cover and named it one of America's best new restaurants in 2015.

Dig into Hola fare and you'll see why. Choose from arepas loaded with shredded beef and plantain, slow-roasted pork, chorizo sausage, and other goodies. Add on black beans, crunchy pickled cabbage, coarse mustard, and cotija cheese that combine for delightfully contrasting flavors and textures. Yet, the menu isn't limited to arepas. Hola also serves up small plates with empanadas, tostadas, fried brussels sprouts, and cauliflower. You'll definitely want to add an order of yucca fries with chimichurri sauce or aioli verde, or both, on the side. On weekends, Hola Arepa is a favorite spot for brunch, too, with a menu heavier on the huevos.

Not surprisingly, Hola Arepa is often jam-packed, but even waiting for a table can be fun in this boisterous hangout, where the weathered wood tables and bright turquoise walls and chairs convey a welcoming tropical feeling. Belly up to the bar and watch as bartenders shake up cocktails that have a Latin flair. Try, for example, the "Sun Down, High Tide," a creative concoction of cognac, pisco, dry curacao, apple-cider grenadine, allspice dram, lemon, and pineapple. Hola also serves beer, wine, seasonal sangria, and soda.

In warm weather, Hola Arepa expands by opening its walls to the outdoors and serving diners and drinkers on its large dog-friendly patio. It also holds the occasional party in its parking lot. Fun as the restaurant is, you'll still want to stop by that Hola Arepa food truck when you see it parked on the streets of Minneapolis and St. Paul

Top right: Hola Arepa serves colorful Latin street food.

Above left: Hola Arepa began as a food truck but now also resides on Nicollet Avenue in Minneapolis.

Above center: Venezuelan arepas are small pancake-like disks made from cornmeal dough stuffed with meat and other goodies. This arrives with a side of yucca fries and bright chimichurri sauce.

Above right: Bartenders mix drinks just right for Hola Arepa's festive atmosphere.

April through October. Follow it on Twitter or Facebook to keep tabs on the truck's location and on the Hola Arepa team's new southeast Asian eatery, Hai Hai (haihaimpls.com) at 2121 University Avenue in northeast Minneapolis.

3501 Nicollet Ave. S., Minneapolis
612-345-5583
holaarepa.com

HOLY LAND

Holy Land has been the Minneapolis mecca of Middle Eastern food since 1986. The Wadi family started the business in a small storefront and expanded over the years as word of its fresh-baked pita, spit-roasted meats, and other Mediterranean delights spread. Even if you don't know your falafel from your kufta or your baba ghanoush from tabouleh, you'll enjoy a walk through Holy Land's colorful aisles of exotic groceries. It has gradually added to the inventory to reflect the neighborhood's changing ethnic complexity and to please gourmet cooks of every stripe.

Shopping at Holy Land is like a mini expedition through Middle Eastern and Mediterranean countries. It offers entire sections piled high with imported cheeses and olives, vast selections of olive oil, and rice of every variety. The meat section displays halal butchered meats and poultry that has been grain fed and farm raised. You'll encounter Middle Eastern pastries and a bazaar of fragrant spices that includes Holy Land-brand spices at prices far below those of a typical grocery store. Workers bake fresh pita bread (sold alongside East African, Ethiopian, Somalian, and Indian breads) and make a Holy Land line of hummus sold both here and in grocery stores and specialty shops.

Over on Holy Land's deli side, you'll see all these ingredients come to life in dishes created from the recipes of family matriarch Mama Fatima. Watch friendly cooks at work in the grilling area, where wood-fired grills blaze, rotisseries revolve roasting whole chickens over the fire, and towers of gyros, beef, chicken, and lamb shawarma turn on spits. There's plenty on the menu for vegetarians, too, including hearty Greek salad and grape leaves stuffed with rice, parsley, tomato, mint, and herbs. Fortunately, combo platters with samples of several dishes make it easy to order without really making up your mind. Load up your produce and deli items to take home, or eat in the dining area accompanied by piped-in Middle Eastern music. It also offers larger quantities of many menu items to cater parties.

Top right: Grilling meats for Middle Eastern dishes to carry out or eat in.

Above left: Holy Land has locations here on Central Avenue and in Midtown Global Market.

Above right: Holy Land stocks many varieties of imported olives and cheeses.

Holy Land's success has planted the seed for other businesses on Central Avenue, including a growing array of other great restaurants to investigate while you're in the neighborhood. Holy Land is open daily from 9:00 a.m. to 9:00 p.m. Hours vary on holidays. See also the branch at Midtown Global Market.

2513 Central Ave. NE, Minneapolis
612-781-2627
holylandbrand.com

Ingebretsen's has been a bastion of all things Scandinavian since 1921. Originally called the Model Meat Market, the business catered to the Scandinavian immigrants who clustered near Lake Street upon arrival in Minneapolis. Those Swedes, Norwegians, Finns, Danes, and Icelanders eventually scattered to other parts of the city and suburbs but have remained loyal to this establishment. As with previous generations, they return to Ingebretsen's for specialty foods and other merchandise that are an important and fun part of their cultural traditions. At Christmas, the line of Scandinavians often extends out the door and along the sidewalk.

Nowhere else will they find such an extensive selection of Danish, Norwegian, and Swedish sausages snuggled into the meat case among the many other meat products Ingebretsen's makes on-site. As with old-fashioned meat markets, friendly butchers preside over the counter, happy to tell you about the home-smoked ham, bacon and spekekjott, (dried meats). Ingebretsen's sells hundreds of pounds of its famous Swedish meatball mix and the gravy to serve with it, along with lingonberries on the side for color.

Ingebretsen's is also the place for that odd yet enduring specialty, lutefisk. For those unfamiliar with one of the more unusual and (to some) unappealing Twin Cities eats, lutefisk is dried cod, usually from Norway, that is rehydrated, originally by soaking it in a lye solution, though processors now use a different chemical solution. The process results in a gelatinous white fish that many claim is tasty when baked and topped with butter. Those crazy Vikings!

Also on the food side of Ingebretsen's shop, you'll find cases of imported cheeses—Danish bleu to Jarlsberg and every sort of havarti—and specialty Scandinavian deli items made daily. Rows and rows of colorful boxes, cans, and jars of imported delicacies fill the surrounding shelves, with a giant wooden Viking statue overseeing the whole operation.

For those who aren't in the hunt for Scandinavian food, the gift shop side of the store offers an array of lovely merchandise. Finnish crystal sparkles on shelves alongside Danish porcelain and Icelandic ceramics. Sterling jewelry from Norway rests near linens from Sweden. Ingebretsen's also took over space in an adjacent building,

Top right: Ingebretsen's has been a Minneapolis institution since 1921.

Above left: Imported cheeses with a Scandinavian focus.

Above center: Friendly butchers sell specialty meat, house-made sausages, and that Scandinavian delicacy, lutefisk.

Above right: Ingebretsen's is the place to stock a Scandinavian pantry and get a little advice on making authentic Swedish meatballs.

where it holds needlework and other classes in Nordic crafts and culture that will have you saying a delighted "Uff da!" even if there's not a drop of Scandinavian blood in your veins.

1601 E. Lake St., Minneapolis

612-729-9333

ingebretsens.com

IZZY'S ICE CREAM

Before passionate ice-cream lovers Lara Hammel and Jeff Sommers opened their ice-cream shop, they immersed themselves in the world of ice cream. They shadowed gelato and ice-cream makers and spent hours crafting their creamy skills to make the perfect frozen delight. The result: Izzy's Ice Cream, with a rotating list of more than 150 flavors.

Every cone comes topped with an "izzy"—an extra ¾-ounce scoop that offers a chance to taste one more flavor. At any given time, thirty-two varieties are on hand at the company's two shops, including classics such as butter pecan, chocolate, and praline pecan. More unusual "signature flavors" include basil, ginger, Guinness, and Swedish Garden Party. "Mix ins" may have M&Ms, Milky Way or Butterfinger bars, and more. Izzy's reports that salted caramel is the overall best-seller. Still, there's plenty of love for Birchwood Key Lime Pie (made with local company Birchwood Café's real key lime pie), Hot Brown Sugar (caramelized brown sugar base with praline pecans toasted in cayenne pepper mixed in), and Irish Moxie (coffee and Jameson Irish whiskey ice-cream base with Heath bars and Oreos mixed in).

If you can limit yourself to one, Izzy's website allows you to sign up for a favorite flavor and receive an email notice when it's available. Izzy's Ice Cream can also be found in many restaurants and grocery stores.

1100 S. Second St., Minneapolis
612-206-3356

2034 Marshall Ave., St. Paul
651-603-1458

izzysicecream.com

Top right: Izzy's Minneapolis location near downtown

Above left: That tiny scoop on top is the "Izzy Scoop."

Above center: Izzy's ice cream is available in more than 150 flavors.

Above right: Izzy's original St. Paul location.

JAX CAFE

Jax is the sort of place where you can imagine Don Draper and his fellow Mad Men and women settling in for a night of cocktail-fueled business deals and romance. Now, Jax doesn't allow those cigarettes that were puffed in the 1950s and '60s, but it still imprints personalized matchbooks before guests arrive. Sinatra-era lounge music wafts through the dining rooms, with a pianist who entertains at the main dining room's grand piano on weekends. It's a huge restaurant, with rooms for weddings and large parties as well as a more intimate bar area.

Family owned since 1933, it proudly retains the white tablecloth supper club style—think paneled walls, rose-patterned carpet, and velvet curtains—that has made it a favorite of the Nordeast neighborhood for generations. The menu reflects that style too. Pierogis, cabbage rolls, Polish sausage links, and sauerkraut are all reminders of the Eastern European heritage of the neighborhood, but more standard supper club classics also abound, including the Waldorf salad and Steak House Wedge of iceberg lettuce. Diners slice into steaks and chops that arrive on sizzling platters, as well as prime rib, crab legs, shrimp, and lobster tail. Trout is on the menu, too, which you may net yourself from the little stream on Jax's beautifully planted garden patio in warm weather.

1928 University Ave., Minneapolis
612-789-7297
jaxcafe.com

Top left: Netting a trout for dinner from the stream on Jax's outdoor patio. Photo by Jax Café

Top right: Jax is proud of its classic supper club feel. Photo by Jax Café

Above left: Pierogi reflect the Eastern European heritage of Jax's northeast Minneapolis neighborhood.

Above right: Classic steak and lobster at Jax. Photo by Jax Café

KITCHEN WINDOW

If you love cooking—and eating!—you'll be dazzled when you step into Kitchen Window, Uptown Minneapolis's mecca of cooking supplies. Here you'll find twenty-thousand square feet of cookware, cutlery, espresso machines, high-end European chocolate, sauces, exotic spices, ingredients for ethnic cooking, and mixes and syrups to craft your own cocktails—literally anything you can think of that has to do with cooking and even a few things you haven't thought of.

The knowledgeable staff is happy to share information on products and cooking tips, even if you don't buy a thing. Like car shopping, fans of outdoor grilling will enjoy having a look at the grills that range from standard charcoal models to Big Green Eggs to big shiny grills the size of small cars. You can't kick the tires, but in summer you can take a test-drive of sorts and learn the intricacies of grilling and smoking at classes on Kitchen Window's outdoor patio. Other classes in its huge state-of-the-art classrooms cover everything from the most basic skills and simple weeknight dinners to more advanced cooking and Italian wine dinners, for example. After class, students sit back with fellow cooks to sip beer or wine and consume the fruits of their labor. Kitchen Window rents equipment and will find you a chef to hire too.

3001 Hennepin Ave., Minneapolis
612-824-4417
kitchenwindow.com

Top right: Making meringues at Kitchen Window cooking school.

Above left: Raspberry pavlova with vanilla cream cheese mousse, part of a Valentine's Day Dinner cooking class at Kitchen Window.

Above right: Learning to make lobster tostadas.

KRAMARCZUK'S SAUSAGE COMPANY

A Nordeast Minneapolis institution, Kramarczuk's is a caféteria-style restaurant, deli, butcher shop, bakery, and retailer of old-world specialties. Honored by the James Beard Foundation as one of America's Classics and featured on cable TV's *Diners, Drive-Ins and Dives* and *Food Paradise*, Kramarczuk's offers delicious, authentic Eastern European fare in a comfortable, casual setting.

Founded in 1954 by a refugee Ukrainian sausage maker and his wife, Kramarczuk's is famous for its forty-plus varieties of handcrafted sausage, from traditional old-world specialties to tangy Cajun, French, and Italian links—tantalizingly arrayed in the deli case or grilled and served hot, and laden with sauerkraut, in their restaurant. Other savory Ukrainian dishes, all made from scratch on the premises, include varenyky (meat, cheese, and potato pierogis), piroshok (bread roll filled with meat, mushrooms, and hard-boiled eggs), holubets (stuffed cabbage rolls), Ukrainian meatballs, goulash,

Affectionately known among locals as Nordeast, Minneapolis's northeast side is a working-class neighborhood rich in immigrant traditions. Nordeast owes its existence to the lumber and grain mills erected in the mid-1800s on the banks of the Mississippi River, downstream from Minnesota's northern pine forests and wheat farms and adjacent to St. Anthony Falls' hydropower. Waves of Polish, Ukrainian, Russian, German, Finnish, Serbian, and Slovak immigrants soon flocked to Nordeast's factories and built homes and churches there.

Kramarczuk's serves beer from Germany and Eastern Europe.

As late as 1930, more than half of "Nordeasterners" were immigrants. Though much of its former industrial base has faded, Nordeast today boasts a flourishing cultural scene, including hundreds of art galleries and artists' studios, the recently renovated Ritz Theater, and a plethora of new and eclectic restaurants, bars, and clubs. But its Eastern European, blue-collar heritage continues to define this unique, vibrant community.

and borscht. For indecisive diners, the combination plate—grilled sausage, varenyky, holubets, and sauerkraut—offers the best of all worlds. Kramarczuk's unique beer card features hard-to-find German, Baltic, and Polish brews, plus a few domestic quaffs.

At Kramarczuk's bakery, freshly baked babkas, old-world breads, and mouthwatering Ukrainian cookies, pastries, and cakes are on full display. The deli features made-to-order salami, ham, turkey, pastrami, and krakowska (a type of Polish sausage) sandwiches, delicious cuts of beef and pork, and imported specialty sauces, jams, chocolates, and crackers. Kramarczuk's is open seven days a week, and the restaurant is first come, first served. Free parking is available next to the store, and area street and ramp parking are also available.

215 E. Hennepin Ave., Minneapolis
612-379-3018
kramarczuks.com

Top: Kramarczuk's is a bastion of its Nordeast neighborhood.

Above left: Piles of Polish are just part of the house-made sausage selection.

Above right: Brats, borscht, and bread to eat in Kramarczuk's restaurant.

MATT'S BAR VERSUS THE 5-8 CLUB

The Great Burger Battle

Nothing—not politics, religion, or anything else—more bitterly splits normally mild-mannered Twin Citians than whether Matt's Bar or the 5-8 Club makes the better melted cheese-stuffed hamburger, called the "Jucy Lucy" at Matt's and the "Juicy Lucy" at 5-8. Over this Great Burger Divide, families have been torn asunder, close friendships severed, and political allegiances abandoned. Without taking either side—the hate mail from the losing camp's devotees would be overwhelming—the cult of the "JL" (as we'll generically refer to it here) and each establishment's claim to it is one of the Cities' fascinating food sagas.

Simply stated, a classic JL consists of two ground beef patties, sealed together at their edges, with a generous dollop of American cheese imprisoned between them. When grilled to medium-well, the cheese assumes the consistency and temperature of tongue-burning lava. Adorned with sliced pickles, grilled onions, and a bakery bun, the JL is one of life's great guilty pleasures, and both Matt's and 5-8 sell them in prodigious numbers.

Both establishments have garnered local and national acclaim for their JLs. Among other honors, both have been featured on the Travel Channel's *Food Wars* and Adam Richman's *Man v. Food*. The Travel Channel listed the 5-8 Club #1 among "America's 101 Tastiest Places to Chow Down" in 2014, while that same year President Barack Obama sampled Matt's Jucy Lucy and proclaimed it "a great burger." They routinely swap "Best Burger" awards from several Twin Cities food-and-drink magazines and polls.

Yet, the two sport decidedly different personalities and atmospheres. The 5-8 Club is a bar, grill, and restaurant, serving in addition to its Juicy Lucy a variety of appetizers, salads, chili, specialty burgers and other sandwiches, wings, dinner baskets, and desserts. The 5-8 also offers several variations on its Juicy Lucy,

Left: Matt's Bar in Minneapolis is one of two bars that claim to have invented the Jucy Lucy burger.

Right: The 5-8 Club's Juicy Lucy, a famous burger with a molten cheese center.

including other cheese fillings, cheese-and-bacon interiors, and even the PB&J—two patties stuffed with cheese and peanut butter and topped with strawberry jam. Such tinkerings are heresy at Matt's, a classic, dimly lit Upper Midwest neighborhood bar; its Jucy Lucys come in one flavor, and basic hamburgers and cheeseburgers, grilled chicken and ham-and-cheese sandwiches, and fries complete the menu. Both offer a range of craft, domestic, and imported beers, on tap and in bottles, plus wine and cocktails.

So who wins the battle of the burgers? Try 'em both—you decide. You won't go wrong either way.

Matt's Bar
3500 Cedar Ave. S., Minneapolis
612-722-7072
mattsbar.com

The 5-8 Club
5800 Cedar Ave. S., Minneapolis
612-823-5858
5-8club.com

MERLINS REST PUB

Sure, many British pubs claim to be "authentic," but do they boast of four-hundred-plus different Scotch and Irish whiskeys behind the bar? Or sport their own minister of culture, keeper and purveyor of all things Celtic? Or offer wildly popular scotch tastings, celebrations of English food, live entertainment, pub trivia challenges, bawdy and G-rated sing-alongs, and similar events on a weekly or monthly basis? Selected by local diners as City Pages' Best Minneapolis Pub in 2016, Merlins Rest brings hearty food and drink, truly authentic atmosphere, and a rollicking good time to Minneapolis's thriving East Side food-and-drink scene.

The menu features classic, tasty pub fare, including fish and chips, bangers and mash, Yorkshire pudding, a variety of meat- and veggie-filled pies and pasties, beefy stews, an ample ploughman's plate, Scotch eggs, and other traditional pub offerings. Diners less loyal to the Crown can also partake of a variety of burgers, sandwiches, wraps, salads, and soups. Tap beers include most of the usual British and Irish suspects, including stouts, porters, Irish and Scottish ales, and ciders, plus a nice selection of local craft brews. Merlins Rest also offers classic specialty cocktails and a modest selection of red, white, and sparkling wines.

But it's the whiskey card, ensconced in the famed Whiskey Bible, that truly distinguishes Merlins Rest from its Celtic competitors. Easily the most comprehensive list of Scotch and Irish whiskeys around, the Whiskey Bible challenges novices and aficionados alike with a mind-blowing array of brown spirits, ranging from light, sweet Lowlands and rich Speyside and Highlands to dark, smoky, peaty Islays, all in varying amounts and prices. Knowledgeable bartenders and serving staff cheerfully provide overwhelmed patrons with suggestions and samplings to suit both palate and budget. Single-malt scotch tastings occur on the first Thursday evening of each month and are by reservation only; slots fill up quickly.

Merlins Rest also features live Celtic, jazz, folk, and other music, plus open-to-all Celtic jam sessions, pub games, organized sing-alongs, and similar events; a full monthly schedule appears on

Top right: Merlins Rest has a comprehensive list of Scotch and Irish whiskeys sold by the dram.

Above left: Bill Watkins, Merlin's Rest minister of culture.

Above right: Shepherd's pie is a hearty treat on a winter night.

Merlins Rest's website. Families with children are common during early evenings, and no visit to Merlins Rest would be complete without a convivial chat with its minister of culture, noted Celtic author "Wild" Bill Watkins, often enthroned near the bar in full kilt and dagger. Except for some special events, reservations are not accepted, and street parking is available.

3601 E. Lake St., Minneapolis

612-216-2419

merlinsrest.com

MERITAGE

Say "bonjour" to Meritage, St. Paul's version of the classic French brasserie-style restaurant. Dining at Meritage (a name that merges merit and heritage) seems a bit like a trip to France, only without the passport and with much friendlier Midwestern service. If you detect a bit of romance in the air, perhaps it's because Meritage's owners had their wedding in this space and later made it their own.

It's one of the Cities' most highly regarded eateries, and chef/owner Russell Klein has received many James Beard Award nominations. There's a classic fin de siécle-style bar area—think big mirrors and zinc bar—and a larger, very atmospheric dining room. The menu changes frequently but continuously offers a traditional oyster bar with an impressive variety of oysters and a selection of other fruits de mer. Hors d'oeuvres include steak tartare, escargot in garlic-parsley butter, and marinated grilled quail with duck confit—très elegant. Entrées walk the line between classic French fare and innovative modern cuisine, with the common element of ultrafresh and local ingredients and precise preparation. So, you'll find moules frites; traditional cassoulet with a ragout of white beans, garlic sausage, and pork and duck confit; and steak au poivre. Yet, the menu may also offer squash and wild mushroom risotto and a house hamburger that's unlike most burgers in the US or France, with garlic aioli, Emmanthaler cheese, and shallot confit. As you'd expect, the wine list emphasizes French wines and domestic wines in the French style, with a few Spanish and Italian selections too. For a complete experience, the kitchen prepares a five- to nine-course tasting menu, with or without wine pairings.

The sidewalk outside Meritage becomes a sidewalk café in summer with a view of Rice Park. Keep an eye out for this eatery's special events, such as its bivalve celebration, Oysterfest, in fall. Though Meritage is a destination in its own right, its downtown St. Paul location makes it a great spot for pre-event dining. The Park Square Theater and Vieux Carré jazz club are downstairs in the same building, and Meritage isn't far from the Ordway Music Theater, the Fitzgerald Theater, the Palace Theatre, or maybe even a wild hockey game at Xcel Energy Center.

Top right: Baskets of crunchy baguettes and other bread.

Above left: The dining room looks out on St. Paul's Rice Park.

Above center: "Fruits de Mer" include shrimp, crab, oysters, and mussels. Photo by: Travis Anderson

Above right: Classic French cassoulet is a Meritage standard. Photo by: Travis Anderson

Meritage is open for lunch Tuesday through Friday, dinner Tuesday through Sunday, and brunch on Saturday and Sunday.

410 Saint Peter St., St. Paul
651-222-5670
meritage-stp.com

MICKEY'S DINER

Looking for a casual dining spot that's (1) listed on the National Register of Historic Places, (2) featured in several full-length motion pictures, and (3) been in continuous operation, 24/7/365, since before World War II? Welcome to the iconic Mickey's Diner, one of the few original classic dining cars still in operation in the Midwest and a downtown St. Paul institution.

Mickey's dining car—manufactured in New Jersey in 1937 and opened to hungry St. Paulites in 1939—is an architectural gem. Its red-and-yellow exterior, closely resembling a railroad dining car of that era, sports wide train-style windows and brightly lit Art Deco signage. Inside, four booths and seventeen stools snugly adjoin a long serving counter with griddles, grills, coffee urns, Mixmasters, and virtually every other kitchen accoutrement known to man carefully clustered behind the counter. Mickey's charmingly sassy and irreverent cooks and servers add to the '30s ambiance. It's no wonder that Mickey's is a favorite location of Hollywood filmmakers and television producers, having been featured in the *Mighty Ducks* movies, *Jingle All the Way, A Prairie Home Companion*, and numerous small-screen productions.

Though offering quintessential short-order fare, Mickey's is no stereotypical greasy spoon. Meats, dairy products, and bakery items are all locally sourced, delicious soups and stews are made in-house from scratch, and the aromatic coffee is ground fresh and roasted locally. You'll find breakfast served 24/7, and Mickey's frisbee-sized buttermilk pancakes, fluffy three-egg omelets, tasty breakfast meats, and crispy hash browns/potatoes O'Brien are legendary. Juicy burgers and grilled sandwiches adorn the lunch and dinner menu along with Mickey's famous bean soup, chili, and Mulligan stew. Full-plate entrées include fish and chips, homemade fried chicken, pork chops, strip steak, and liver and onions. If any gastrointestinal space remains, Mickey's offers up classic hand-dipped shakes and malts and some great apple pie.

Over the years, Mickey's has won accolades as one of America's best diners from such diverse reviewers as *Gourmet*, epicurious.com, the Food Network, and many others. Its loyal fans include everyone from celebrities, politicians, and downtown St. Paul professionals to local

Top right: Great burgers are grilled before your eyes as you sit counterside at Mickey's.

Above left: Mickey's makes thick shakes with real ice cream

Above right: The iconic Mickey's is an authentic diner from the 1930s.

Janes and Joes, history and entertainment buffs, and 3:00 a.m. revelers suffering the munchies. Mickey's honors major credit cards but no checks and does not take reservations, so lines are not uncommon at peak hours. Free parking is available at Mickey's adjoining surface lot, and free and metered street parking lines area streets.

36 W. Seventh St., St. Paul
651-698-0259
mickeysdiningcar.com

MIDTOWN GLOBAL MARKET

East Lake Street in Minneapolis has long been a place where each new wave of immigrants to Minnesota sets up shops and restaurants to establish an economic foothold in their new country. At the center of it all sits Midtown Global Market, a virtual United Nations of food all in one building that was formerly a giant Sears & Roebuck store.

Start your visit with a little reconnaissance mission. Wander through the international shops that sell jewelry, household decor, handicrafts, soaps, and art. Stroll among the more than twenty-five restaurants, bars, and specialty grocers to take in the colors, smells, and activity and see what tempts you. What are you hungry for? Middle Eastern, Indian, Mexican, Scandinavian, Italian, Asian, African? It's all here. If it's a burger you desire, Safari Express will grill up a camel burger. Or, find a more traditional burger-and-fry combo at Andy's Garage.

There's no pretense at Midtown Global Market. Just place an order and eat at tables in the center of the market—accompanied by live entertainment on weekends. Or, take your food to eat in the market's brewhouse, East Lake Brewing and Taphouse, which features its own beer and has kombucha and botanically brewed soda, too. You'll find another great alternative, the full-service Korean gastropub, Rabbit Hole, on the edge of the market.

The specialty grocers at Midtown Global are eager to help home cooks stock their pantries with gourmet goodies and hard-to-find ethnic foods. For example, in addition to prepared meals, the Midtown outpost of Holy Land (see page 78) has a halal butcher counter, grocery shop, and deli. In the market, Grass Roots Gourmet sells regionally produced cheese, meat, and bread, which makes a great gift basket or picnic fare. You can purchase fresh-baked bread and gorgeous sweet treats at the headquarters of the award-winning Salty Tart bakery (see page 152).

Kitchen in the Market holds many cooking classes taught by local chefs and food artisans. It creates interesting themed experiences, such as "Psychic Suppers," with cooking and psychic readings. Or,

Top right: Diners may purchase food from the market's many vendors and take it home or eat in the central dining area.

Above left: Midtown Global Market is located on a great bike trail, the Midtown Greenway, and makes an excellent stop to purchase picnic supplies.

Above right: Fresh fruit and vegetables for sale at Midtown Global Market.

students at the "Cooking the Market" class start with appetizers and a champagne cocktail and then tour the market to gather interesting ingredients they then cook and eat.

Midtown Global Market is easily accessible by bike from the Midtown Greenway, a cycling and walking path that runs adjacent to the market.

920 E. Lake St., Minneapolis
612-872-4041
midtownglobalmarket.org

MILKJAM CREAMERY

Milkjam's intense and unique combinations of flavor, color, and texture make it one of Minneapolis's most popular ice-cream emporiums. House favorites include the aptly named Black, made from the darkest chocolate and almost fudge-like in appearance and texture, and Milkjam itself, an ultrarich blend of three caramelized milks (goat's, cow's, and condensed). Other regular offerings are Thai Tea (aromatic black tea with condensed milk), Cereal Killers (orange coriander milk with candied pebbles), and Poppin' Bottles (champagne sorbet; expect to show your ID). Selections change frequently, though, so don't be surprised to encounter Indian Elvis (curry, peanut butter, and banana), Spicy Pineapple (pineapple with Thai chilies), or dozens of others. Names sometimes vary. During National Women's History Month, for instance, Black becomes "The Notorious R.B.G.," and Milkjam morphs to "Beyonce."

Milkjam also features decadent sundae specials (e.g., the "Dear Mama," made with Milkjam ice cream, rose meringue, kataifi, pistachios, and rose petals), the "Jam Bun" (an ice-cream sandwich made with Glam Doll doughnuts), and adult floats containing sparkling wine, beer, or Lambic. For the incurably indecisive, Milkjam offers the "All of Them" sundae, a beautiful arrangement of one scoop of everything in the store, with an assortment of toppings and garnishes.

2743 Lyndale Ave. S., Minneapolis
612-424-4668
milkjamcreamery.com

Top right: Ice-cream sandwiches come with ice cream inside a Glam Doll doughnut.

Above left: Milkjam offers a rotating list of amazing ice-cream flavors. Some are vegan

Above center: A universal sentiment at Milkjam Creamery.

Above right: Colorful and creatively named treats.

MINNESOTA STATE FAIR

The first Minnesota State Fair took place in 1859, one year after Minnesota became a state. Since then, the Great Minnesota Get-Together has grown to become one of the state's most beloved traditions. It's the largest state fair in the United States by average daily attendance, with as many as 1.9 million people flocking in over twelve days.

The original purpose of the fair was to showcase the many achievements of Minnesota agriculture. You won't find as many tractors and combines displayed on Machinery Hill anymore, but folks from all over the state still come to the fair to show off their animals, produce, and homemaking skills. You'll also find art, handicrafts, rodeos, concerts, rides on the midway, parades, and entertainment of every form. The Department of Natural Resources booth offers an encounter with local flora and fauna, TV and radio stations broadcast live, and the state's politicians show up to meet and greet constituents.

Still, to a great extent, the fair is about food—growing it, cooking it, and most of all eating it. Competitions abound for every sort of baking, canning, pickling, and other type of food preparation. Even some of the artwork is fashioned from food, as in the case of the dairy queen, Princess Kay of the Milky Way, whose likeness is annually carved from a ninety-pound block of butter.

This feeding frenzy offers nearly five hundred foods at three hundred food concessions. Some healthy food exists, but really, why try? It's easier to abandon yourself to candied bacon, Twinkies, spaghetti and meatballs, candy bars, key lime pie, corn dogs, walleye, and pork chops, all deep fried and served on a stick. No trip to the fair is complete without mini doughnuts and a bucket of Sweet Martha's cookies. Wash them down with all the milk you can drink for two dollars at the Milk Stand. Or head to the "Land of 10,000 Beers" Craft Beer Hall, where the Minnesota Craft Brewers Guild presents some of the state's best brews and hard cider.

To make a dent in the dining fare, you need a plan, so grab one of the food and dining directories by the gates, and remember to avoid the rides and the Miracle of Birth Barn on a full stomach.

Top right: The State Fair is known for the many foods served on a stick, such as corn dogs. Photo by Minnesota State Fair

Above left: At the Milk Stand, all you can drink for two dollars. Photo by Minnesota State Fair

Above center: The Minnesota State Fair attracts more than 1.9 million visitors annually. Photo by Minnesota State Fair

Above right: A bucket full of Sweet Martha's cookies tops a day of eating. Photo by Sweet Martha's Cookies

The fair runs for twelve consecutive days from late August into early September, ending on Labor Day.

Minnesota State Fairgrounds
1265 Snelling Ave. N., St. Paul
651-288-4400
mnstatefair.org

MOSCOW ON THE HILL

The rosy, dimly lit rooms at Moscow on the Hill seem like the perfect place for international intrigue, romance, or reminiscences about the old country. Okay, this is St. Paul, not Moscow, and it's much closer to the Mississippi River than to the Volga, but the combination of Russian food, vodka, and conviviality will set your imagination in motion nonetheless.

Pick a seat at the Vodka Bar, which offers a seemingly endless array billed as the largest vodka selection in the US, and raise your shot glass with a toast, "na zdorovie," to your health. Or settle into one of the gauze-draped dining rooms for a meal that's often accompanied by accordion music and the songs and table pounding of fellow diners. The menu offers appetizers, such as blini with caviar, beef and cabbage piroshkis, Russian herring, and steaming cups of borscht soup. Entrée favorites range from authentic dumplings and cabbage rolls to beef stroganoff and plates of shashlik, a.k.a. shish kebabs. Cap off your meal with cheese blintzes or White Russian tiramisu.

When Moscow on the Hill thaws out in summer, it opens the lovely patio in back.

Open for brunch, lunch, and dinner year-round, including holidays.

371 Selby Ave., St. Paul
651-291-1236
moscowonthehill.com

Top: Diners at Moscow on the Hill enjoy a great patio in summer and Eastern European music year-round. Photo by Moscow on the Hill

Above left: Moscow on the Hill in St. Paul features an extensive selection of vodka and traditional Russian food. Photo by Moscow on the Hill

Above right: Siberian Pelmeni, Moscow on the Hill's handmade dumplings. Photo by Moscow on the Hill

MURRAY'S

Murray's opened in 1946, and the "new" red neon Murray's sign, added in 1954, has been an iconic beacon leading diners to Sixth Street in downtown Minneapolis ever since. Some things have changed. There's no Murray's Orchestra serenading diners, and the $1.25 steak dinner is long gone, but the Murray family's third generation runs its beef-centric eatery with the same pride and quality as their grandparents. Murray's menu offers a nice selection of seafood—potato chip-crusted walleye, blackened salmon, asiago halibut—and lovely salads of roasted beets, spinach, mixed greens, and the classic '50s iceberg wedge. Let's face it, though, Murray's is all about meat. Murray's beef, cut by in-house meat cutters, comes in just about every cut—New York strip, porterhouse, ribeye, hangar steak—and may be topped with crusts of blue cheese or peppercorn, bearnaise sauce, or add-ons of lobster tail, shrimp, and more. You'll also see chateaubriand for two and the restaurant's piece de résistance, the twenty-eight-ounce Silver Butter Knife Steak (also hopefully for two). Murray's lunch menu and bar offerings cater to less gargantuan appetites and to those seeking quick bites, especially great for anyone on their way to Twins, Vikings, Timberwolves, or Lynx games, all close to Murray's.

26 S. Sixth St., Minneapolis
612-339-0909
murraysrestaurant.com

Above left: The famous Silver Butter Knife Steak for two. Photo by Murray's Restaurant

Top right: The third generation of the Murray family continues this eatery's fine dining tradition. Photo by Murray's Restaurant

Above center: Fillets come with elegant extras, such as blue cheese. Photo by Murray's Restaurant

Above right: Though updated, Murray's retains its classic atmosphere. Photo by Murray's Restaurant

ON'S KITCHEN

The family-owned Thai eatery, On's, is a standout among the string of small and interesting eateries along University Avenue and the light rail green line. On Khumchaya herself is in the kitchen of this no-frills establishment chopping fresh veggies and stirring up the recipes that she's been cooking since her childhood in Thailand. The main ornamentation in On's dining room is the little shrine in the corner, but that's okay because the colors, aromas, and textures of the dishes she turns out are as pleasing to the senses as any work of art. Lean in over your food to inhale steam scented with traditional Thai flavors, such as basil, lemongrass, garlic, and curry. Crunch into the super fresh spring rolls, and sip the savory noodle soups with beef or seafood, or perhaps with squid, shrimp, or tofu. You'll find curries and a list of specials that emphasize seafood, such as tilapia, soft shell crab, salmon, and more. The menu is enormous, with all dishes prepared to order, so it's hard to choose. When pressed, On recommends number 90, Pla-Lad-Prik, which is deep-fried fillet of tilapia topped with curry seasoning. "What is that incredible spice I'm tasting?" you may ask. "Mom won't give out her recipes," laughs the server, so you'll have to keep coming back. Dine in or take out. Open 9:00 a.m. to 9:00 p.m., Tuesday through Saturday.

1613 University Ave., St. Paul
651-644-1444
onskitchen.com

Top right: Fresh, crunchy Thai spring rolls.

Above left: A small shrine at On's Kitchen.

Above right: Pad-Ga-Prow, stir-fried beef with basil and chili peppers.

PIMENTO

Reggae music sets the mood as you enter this fun and mellow bit of Kingston, Jamaica, on Eat Street, Minneapolis, where the motto is "Don't Worry. Eat Happy." At Pimento, decorated with sunny yellow walls and green trim (the colors of the Jamaican flag), you can't help but feel both your mood and your appetite rise as you line up at the counter to order your food.

Pimento is the brainchild of an unlikely trio of owners—Tomme Beevas, a Jamaica-born businessman; Yoni Reinharz, who was formerly, among other things, a pioneer of Jewish-Jamaican rap music; and the Soviet Union-born Sergey Kogan, who is both an organic hops farmer and a chef trained at Paris's Cordon Bleu. Their menu is simple, based primarily on slow-roasted meats and the recipes of Beevas's grandmother, Sylvia "Baby Lue" Jones. Standards include Kingston-style jerk chicken and slow-roasted pork (with the

Nowhere is ethnic dining more concentrated in Minneapolis than along "Eat Street," a five-block stretch of Nicollet Avenue between Twenty-Fourth and Twenty-Ninth Streets. Eat Street is home to more than forty wildly diverse restaurants, cafés, and other eateries. Got a yen for Asian? You'll find Chinese, Vietnamese, Thai, Malaysian, and Korean. European? Pick from Greek, German, Italian, and French. African? Check. Americas more to your liking? Try out Jamaican, Mexican, Caribbean, and even an American joint or two. Doughnuts, bakeries, and coffee shops complete the list. Most are relatively small, all are welcoming and friendly, and there isn't a chain establishment on the list.

Left: Such dishes as slow-roasted pulled pork come with crispy slaw, sweet grilled plantains, and a choice of sauces, mild to "Kill Dem Wid It" hot.

Right: Line up to order at Pimento and food is delivered to your table in this sunny Eat Street eatery.

two combined in the dish "One Love"). They're served in a bowl with coconut rice and beans, Jamaican slaw, and sweet cooked plantains. Other options include curry dishes and a rotating list of specials that may include sandwiches or roasted goat. The house-made sauces allow for endless variation with each dish, from the Neutralizer with sweet onion and smoked paprika sauce to the Kill Dem Wid It sauce that packs a habanero-filled punch. As in Jamaica, you can cool off with a bottle of Red Stripe beer or Tomboy Guyana and West Indian sodas.

The gang at Pimento likes to host an event now and then, such as their party to watch the Jamaican team in the Olympics. Even better, they're taking the party out back in summer with a new patio that includes an outdoor bar and live music. Open 11:00 a.m. to 10:00 p.m. They're also happy to help you cater a Jamaica-style party.

2524 Nicollet Ave. S., Minneapolis

612-345-5637

pimentokitchen.com

PINKU JAPANESE STREET FOOD

From the time you hit the front door, with its bright yellow graphics, you have a clue that PinKU is not just an ordinary sushi restaurant. PinKU strives to serve traditional, fast, and very fresh food like that found in the street stalls of Japan. A narrow, alley-like thirty-two-seat place with black walls and a giant flowered fish mural, PinKU is stylish, urban, and built for speed.

Dishes on the menu—only ten of them—derive from the cooking style of co-owner John Sugimura's grandmother in Japan. They include variations of salmon, shrimp, tuna, and pot stickers, each artfully prepared in front of you in the open kitchen, and they're delivered to your table, pronto, in little metal trays. Whether it's shrimp on a tiny bed of radish noodles, salmon lightly "kissed" with a blowtorch on crispy rice, or rolls, such as the special crab roll, each dish combines flavors and textures that will make you close your eyes and make yummy sounds. Plates are small, so plan on three per person, minimum. PinKU also features sake, beer, and wine.

Sugimura and co-owner Xiaoteng Huang (a.k.a. "X") intend to perfect this style of fast but high-quality Japanese street food and then quickly expand the business to many other locations. Eat here and you can say you were in on the ground floor.

20 University Ave., Minneapolis
612-584-3167
pinkujapanese.com

Top right: Searing salmon in PinKU's open kitchen.

Above left: PinKU means "pink" in Japanese and connotes peace and democracy.

Above right: Crab rolls, seared salmon, and PinKU's distinctive rice.

PSYCHO SUZI'S MOTOR LOUNGE

Delightfully irreverent and slightly bawdy to boot, Psycho Suzi's boasts one of the most popular and eclectic bar-and-food scenes in the Twin Cities. Start with the non sequitur of a sprawling, multilevel Polynesian-themed tiki bar and restaurant in decidedly untropical Nordeast Minneapolis, in a building that once (ironically) housed a church. Add to it a great riverfront patio overlooking the Mississippi, replete with tiki torches, Easter Island stone heads, and thatched sun canopies, where leashed, well-behaved dogs bring their masters for food and drink on balmy summer evenings. Then tack on the Saturday night Shangri-La cocktail lounge, luring thirsty patrons to the Shrunken Head, Forbidden Cove, or Ports of Pleasure bars and featuring a nifty in-house instrumental jazz group. Adventures in paradise, indeed.

Even the coolest digs, of course, can't survive without tasty food and potent drink, and Psycho Suzi's doesn't disappoint here either. Main dishes include stone-baked or deep-dish pizzas laden with a wide variety of meats, veggies, and sauces; custom burgers; a wonderful Cubano sandwich; and various pasta entrées. It's easy to make a meal out of the appetizers, with cheese curds, tater tots, wings, and brown sugar babies (bacon-wrapped smoky links in a brown sugar and bourbon sauce) among the favorites. Suzi's also offers Sunday brunch (on Saturdays, too, just to be different), consisting mostly of an eclectic variety of egg dishes. There's also the extensive, wildly imaginative cocktail list, running the gamut from traditional Mai Tais and rum punches served in tiki mugs to Leilani's Fire Bowl, described as "48-oz. of liquor-on-fire nonsense . . . a cadre of booze and boozosity" and recommended for consumption by two to four brave souls. An ample selection of local craft beers and wines is also on hand, but it's the tiki drink card that steals the show.

Top everything else off with the hippest, coolest, best-tattooed waitstaff around, and it's easy to see why Psycho Suzi's is a favorite gathering place for locals and visitors alike. Be forewarned that Suzi's only accepts reservations during the day for groups of eight

Left: Psycho Suzi's is famous for its tiki drinks and kitschy tropical atmosphere. Photo by Psycho Suzi's Motor Lounge

Right: One of Minneapolis's favorite patios, Suzi's overlooks the Mississippi River. Photo by Psycho Suzi's Motor Lounge

or more in the restaurant, and that the wait time for a table on the patio on summer weekend nights is often sixty to seventy minutes or even longer. Valet parking is available, or if you're boating on the Mississippi, tie up to the boat dock and climb the short bluff. If you're also visiting Suzi's equally crazy younger sister's place—Betty Danger's Country Club, just three blocks away—a "Tiki Tram" runs between the two in summer months.

1900 Marshall St. NE, Minneapolis
612-788-9069
psychosuzis.com

QUANG

Quang has been introducing folks to the wonders of Vietnamese food for nearly thirty years. It's a big, open, and lively place, where you can expect to be seated at communal tables. That's the fun of it. There's every kind of person eating here, perhaps most notably children. Depending on the time of day, you may feel underdressed without a baby carrier with you. That tells you that all are welcome; come as you are . . . and they pack 'em in.

You'll see Quang diners hunched over, not with bad posture, but with the intent to slurp down some of the city's best bowls of pho (pronouced fuh). That's a noodle soup that originated as street food in Vietnam. It comes in all sorts of ingredient combinations but generally consists of broth, rice noodles, and meat. Don't worry about eating pho with grace. Use chopsticks, ceramic spoons—anything you want—and it's even okay to just put your face down and sip from the bowl.

There's much more on Quang's menu, though, including fresh spring rolls and meal-size noodle salads served in bowls with mixed lettuce, fresh herbs, and veggies and topped with meat, chicken, shrimp, or tofu. Platter entrées range from grilled pork chops to grilled salmon. A favorite: Com Ga Xao, a lemongrass chicken dish with caramelized onions. Accompany the feast with beer, wine, fresh-squeezed sodas, or a beautiful glass of bubble tea.

2719 Nicollet Ave. S., Minneapolis
612-870-4739
quang-restaurant.com

Top: Quang is a big place with an enthusiastic clientele.

Above: You can place a to-go order at Quang or dine in.

BABANI'S KURDISH RESTAURANT Kubay Brinj, rice dumplings filled with ground beef, spices, and parsley and fried to a crispy brown.

VOLSTEAD'S EMPORIUM Vintage drinks from the 1930s top the cocktail menu. Photo by Volstead's Emporium

CAN CAN WONDERLAND Mini golf holes designed by local artists offer surprises—such as this giant pink beast.

THE COMMODORE BAR & RESTAURANT Lobster deviled eggs are among the appetizers at the Commodore.

FARMERS' MARKETS In summer Twin Cities farmers' markets burst with blooms. Look for special winter hours too.

FIKA This open-faced sandwich includes pork and smoked trout sausage, asparagus, fennel, sea bean, citrus crème fraiche, and pine nuts on caraway rye bread. Photo by Jon Dahlin

ZEN BOX IZAKAYA At Zen Box Izakaya, you'll find Chu-hai cocktails, which are drinks typical of izakayas that combine fresh juice, syrups, and liqueurs. Photo by Travis Anderson

GANDHI MAHAL First round from the luncheon buffet at Gandhi Mahal.

TRAVAIL KITCHEN AND AMUSEMENTS Diners receive numerous artful little plates during their prix fixe Travail dinner. Photo by Courtney Perry

HI-LO DINER Main course or dessert—the High-Top is a not-too-sweet doughnut served with sweet or savory toppings. Photo by Eliesa Johnson Photography

THE LEXINGTON The beloved chicken pot pie is still on the menu at the Lex.

PINKU JAPANESE STREET FOOD Such dishes as crispy shrimp on radish noodles and pot stickers arrive on metal trays.

QUANG Com Ga Xao, a lemongrass chicken platter.

SAFARI Crispy sambuzas (Somali samosas) are served with green basbaas sauce and have ground beef and vegetables inside.

TORI RAMEN Salted duck ramen. Dishes at Tori Ramen are made without the typical pork broth.

WORLD STREET KITCHEN Yum Yum rice bowls come with Korean barbecued short ribs, lamb belly, tofu, lemongrass meatballs, or grilled chicken.

HOLY LAND A wide selection of tea imported from around the Middle East.

REVERIE CAFÉ

Most restaurants these days "throw a bone" to vegetarians with at least one entrée or a combination of salads and appetizers to sustain those who eschew meat. Yet, not many Twin Cities eateries are exclusively vegan. Reverie advertises its fare as "plant-based," perhaps to avoid scaring off omnivores, and, indeed, many Reverie diners are "flexitarians." No matter what your food orientation, the fare here is tasty, pretty, and well textured. The daily menu offers breakfast dishes you might find anywhere else, but with vegan substitutions, such as biscuits and gravy with mushroom gravy instead of sausage, polenta rancheros with spicy pinto beans instead of eggs, and the sausage biscuit with vegan "sausage" from Herbivorous Butcher. Likewise, the TLT sandwich tastes pretty much like a BLT but with tempeh. Tempting tacos are filled with pulled jackfruit and po' boys with cauliflower, all very satisfying even to a carnivorous palate.

For drinks, you'll find a coffee bar; specialty beverages, such as kombucha; and more than forty beers and ciders, including a dedicated gluten-free tap. The bohemian, coffee house atmosphere makes Reverie a perfect gathering place to enjoy music from local and national bands, open-mic nights with spoken word poetry and monologue readings, and live painting by local artists. Open seven days a week.

1931 Nicollet Ave. S., Minneapolis
612-353-5252
reveriempls.com

Top right: The "TLT" substitutes tempeh for bacon.

Above left: Reverie serves only "plant-based" food, such as its jackfruit carnitas tacos.

Above right: You'll find coffee, kombucha, and taps with locally brewed beer and cider.

REVIVAL

You can't get much farther from the American South than Minnesota. Yet Revival has imported the classics of Southern cooking to the Twin Cities, fried green tomatoes and all. Revival chef/co-owner Thomas Boemer was born in Minnesota but grew up in the Carolinas, so he knows how to translate the cooking traditions he learned in the South to Midwesterners. After the first bite of crispy fried chicken, Northerners lined up outside Revival in Minneapolis, ready to swap their wild rice for hush puppies and their walleye for shrimp and grits. That eventually led to a second Revival restaurant in St. Paul.

This is fairly heavy fare, so if you're trying these "foreign" foods for the first time, it's good to have a plan. You can't sample everything in one sitting, so plan to return. The fried chicken is a delicious "must," available Southern fried, Tennessee hot (spicy to the Minnesota palate), poultrygeist (seriously hot), or gluten friendly (not free). Crispy, juicy . . . no matter the spice level, people go nuts over it. That doesn't mean you shouldn't explore other entrée options, such as shrimp and grits, braised oxtail, slow-roasted pork shoulder, or country captain chicken with coconut rice, curry gravy, and golden raisins. The St. Paul location offers more in the way of barbecue, but Boemer has plans to add that to the Minneapolis menu too.

The appetizers and sides offer a chance to try more dishes, mysterious and exotic to Northerners and great for vegetarians. Get a look at this list (not to mention the selection of hot sauces) and you'll understand the need to pace yourself—for example, pork rinds, hot Cheetos style; johnnycakes; crispy pig ears; pickled shrimp and pigs feet; and pimento cheese, sometimes called "the caviar of the South." Sides include all the things you'd imagine would appear at a big Southern family dinner: hush puppies, mac and cheese, white cheddar grits, collard greens, and biscuits and sorghum butter, to name only a few. True to the theme of Southern hospitality, servers will help the unitiated parse the choices. You may feel stuffed, but sometimes it's worth it to just loosen your belt a bit and keep going with one of the homespun desserts, especially the banana cream pie.

Revival has a nice beer and wine list in Minneapolis and a full bar

Top right: Fried chicken, hush puppies, black-eyed peas—Southern food at Revival. Photo by Eliesa Johnson

Above left: Owners Nick Rancone and Thomas Boemer outside their mecca of fried chicken and Southern cooking, Revival. Photo by Eliesa Johnson

Above right: At Revival, save room for pecan pie, banana cream pie, and other Southern-style desserts. Photo by Eliesa Johnson

in St. Paul, but a true Southerner might want to accompany a meal with some good 'ol sweet tea. Open for lunch and dinner.

4257 Nicollet Ave., Minneapolis
612-345-4516

525 Selby Ave., St. Paul
651-340-2355

revivalfriedchicken.com

ROSE STREET PATISSERIE AND PATISSERIE 46

With typical Minnesota modesty, the down-to-earth atmosphere
at Rose Street Patisserie and Patisserie 46 belies the stunning
pastries and delectable breads for sale at these sister establishments,
located in Minneapolis's Linden Hills and Kingfield neighborhoods,
respectively. Come as you are, order coffee, pull up a chair with a
friend, and splurge on pastry that is among the best in the world.
For example, at Rose Street, the larger of the two, wood and cement
industrial seating stands in sharp contrast to the cases that display
pastries like giant jewelry boxes. Only the little sign stenciled on
the door and the small plaque on the wall at Rose Street boast chef/
owner John Kraus's status as the first American member of the
prestigious Relais Desserts fraternity of pastry chefs. You will find
miche, a hearty old-world bread made with the finest local grains;
sourdough (plain, olive, and walnut currant); baguettes; breakfast
baked goods, such as muffins, croissants, and scones; cookies; classic
French eclairs; napoleons; cakes; and tarts. Candy confections
include artisan caramels, macaron towers, nougat, and bon bons
galore, and from May to November you'll also find ice cream. The
patisseries also offer sandwiches, tartines, quiche, and salads. The
upstairs balcony at Rose Street Patisserie makes a great place to
linger and treat yourself to another bonbon. Both locations welcome
dogs in their outdoor seating.

Rose Street Patisserie
2811 W. Forty-Third St., Minneapolis
612-259-7921
rosestreet.co

Patisserie 46
4552 Grand Ave. S, Minneapolis
612-354-3257
patisserie46.com

Top: Rose Street baker/owner John Kraus has garnered international recognition, including membership in Relais Desserts.

Above left: Artisan bread and sandwiches, such as this avocado toast, sit on the savory side of the menu.

Above right: Eye-popping pastries and confections at Rose Street Patisserie and Patisserie 46.

SAFARI

Minnesota has the largest Somali population in the United States, and many Somali immigrants make their home in the Twin Cities. This simple restaurant takes diners on a food safari to Somalia and the Horn of Africa with an array of beef, chicken, goat, fish, and shrimp dishes, usually served with rice and "ke'key" homemade pasta. The colorful food comes with hints of clove, curry, cardamom, and cinnamon, which is no surprise considering Somalia's position on the Indian Ocean and along major trade routes. Starters include sambuzas and hummus platters with pita bread. Favorites include Chicken Fantastic with vegetables and coconut-curry cream sauce and the sliced grilled beef that is sautéed with onions and fresh vegetables and served with rice, and often with a fresh whole banana on the side. Save room to sip a beautiful mango laasi or cinnamon-laced Somali tea with your meal. Open daily, 11:00 a.m. to midnight.

3010 Fourth Ave. S., Minneapolis
612-353-5341
safarirestaurant.net

Top right: Service is friendly and fast at Safari.

Above left: Lassi is like a mango smoothie, with dots of strawberry gel.

Above right: Ke'key is Somali pasta, in this case with cheese and chicken.

SAINT DINETTE

Restaurants typically fit into a category—Italian, burger joint, Chinese take-out, retro diner—you get the idea. Yet the delightfully eclectic menu at Saint Dinette defies categorization. If pressed, they describe the fare as following the path of French exploration of North America from Quebec to the Gulf Coast of Mexico, to, as they say, "discover a three-nation, waterborne joie de vivre."

That's a pretty big umbrella under which to create food, and chef Adam Eaton takes it to the limit. So, depending on the season and what's fresh locally, that may include beer-battered fried smelt, pasta topped with mouthwatering lamb ragout and green olives, a killer (and beautiful) bowl of shrimp and grits, or tacos filled with roast pork, pineapple, and crema. Dumplings are a vegetarian option, with goat cheese, kale, and wild mushrooms. Add to that list, perhaps, matzo ball soup or fantastic cheeseburgers, and you pretty much

Today a National Historic District, St. Paul's Lowertown began life in the 1800s as the lower landing to St. Paul from the Mississippi River, hence the name. It became a major warehouse and distribution point for merchandise being shipped on the river but was largely abandoned after the Great Depression. Today, Lowertown lives again, as those warehouses have become lofts, offices, galleries, bars, and eateries with easy access to St. Paul's historic farmers' market, Mears Park (home to the annual Twin Cities Jazz Festival), and the neighboring CHS Field, home of the St. Paul Saints minor league baseball team.

Top right: A salad of tiny veggies looks as though it came straight from the nearby St. Paul Farmers' Market.

Above left: Tacos represent part of Saint Dinette's exploration of North America.

Above right: Colorful shrimp and grits from the opposite end of the Mississippi from St. Paul.

give up trying to fit the food into any category, but who cares when you're having this much fun. Desserts may include seasonal sorbet, churros, tres leches cake, or the unusual but fantastic crème brûlée that contains a hint of foie gras.

Saint Dinette is located in the Rayette Lofts building, and the dining room's huge windows look out onto the surrounding historic neighborhood. Its casual decor blends the industrial look of the old building's open ductwork and exposed brick with white shell chairs à la the 1960s. You can watch bartenders shaking up creative cocktails at the bar, and they also serve wine and a list of beer that reflects the North America journey, with local brews as well as Canadian and Mexican lagers. The resturant is open Tuesday through Friday, 5:00 p.m. to 10:00 p.m., and open earlier at 10:00 a.m. for brunch on Saturday and Sunday. Saint Dinette will even hold your perishable farmers' market produce in cold storage while you eat.

261 E. Fifth St., St. Paul
651-800-1415
saintdinette.com

SAINT GENEVIEVE

No sane traveler would ever mistake Minneapolis for Paris, but diners at Saint Genevieve can be forgiven for imagining that they've been magically whisked away to a cozy Rive Gauche buvette. Named as one of America's Best New Restaurants in 2016 by *Bon Appetit*, and featured in *Vogue*, the *New York Times*, and other publications, Saint Genevieve brings classic and modern French cuisine, a sumptuous carte des vins, free-flowing champagne, and a distinctly Parisian vibe to south Minneapolis's charming Lynnhurst neighborhood.

Expertly crafted by Saint Genevieve's chef/owner Steven Brown, a two-time James Beard nominee, the diverse menu features a combination of delectable small plates, classic French bistro entrées, and scrumptious tartines. Among the petit plats, guests may savor a gem lettuce salad with fine herbs, emmentaler cheese and a soft-boiled egg; gnocchi with lamb ragout; mussels in a wine-and-herb broth; whole quail with parsnip-mushroom stuffing; and knife-prepared steak tartare. Plats principaux include trout meuniére, choucroute with pork, bratwurst and sauerkraut, steak au poivre, Moroccan chicken, and pan-seared scallops. Saint Genevieve's out-of-this-world tartines range from the classic madame (Spanish ham, raclette, and sunny-side-up egg) and escargot with gruyere and roasted mushrooms to caramelized onion, beet-cured salmon, and ribeye steak creations. Midafternoon and late-night diners (the kitchen is open until midnight, seven days a week) can choose from a subset of dinner offerings, and a separate lunch/brunch menu adds quiches, soups, omelets, and—mais oui!—an American cheeseburger to the midday list. The menu varies seasonally, and new specials arrive regularly. For libations, champagne-aholics will find seven distinctive choices available by the glass and bottle plus an extensive selection of wonderful French reds and whites.

Saint Genevieve's interior is chic, inviting, and unpretentious. Floor-to-ceiling windows and French doors visually connect the restaurant to the neighborhood. In warmer months, the French doors open wide to create another Parisian treasure—the outdoor café. Sip a glass of full-bodied Bordeaux, a fruity white Burgundy, or a Minnesota craft beer with a loved one or friends, snack on a plate of

Top right: Saumon d'ete tartine, piled with beet-cured salmon, deviled egg, snap peas, and fromage blanc. Photo by Fresh Coast Collective

Above left: A Saint Genevieve scallop small plate. Photo by Fresh Coast Collective

Above right: Champagne is ready for tasting by the glass. Photo by Fresh Coast Collective

frites, and celebrate la joie de vivre. Also look for Saint Genevieve's popular special events, including Sunday salons and wine tastings, holiday tasting menus, and champagne and wine dinners.

Dinner reservations are highly recommended, though patient walk-ins can dine off the full menu at Saint Genevieve's bar when a stool becomes available. Ample parking can be found on neighborhood streets.

5003 Bryant Ave. S., Minneapolis
612-353-4843
stgmpls.com

SAINT PAUL GRILL

Fold up your *Wall Street Journal* and settle into one of the booths at the St. Paul Grill. Located in the venerable St. Paul Hotel, this classic eatery makes a perfect meeting place for a power lunch or business dinner. Yet, in an era of super casual neighborhood dining spots and fewer white-tablecloth venues, the St. Paul Grill stands out as a lovely alternative for the non-business crowd, too. Its mahogany paneling, patterned carpets, and huge windows that look out on Rice Park (an especially nice view when decorated with ice sculptures during the St. Paul Winter Carnival) make this a prime spot for a romantic dinner or, with the Ordway Music Theater just across the park, a pre-theater nosh.

White-aproned servers guide diners through the menu, which specializes in classic upscale grill fare. The extensive dinner menu offers starters of escargot, ahi tuna, crab cakes, calamari, and even slices of bacon. Among entrées, steaks, prime rib, and thick-cut chops abound along with chicken, duck breast, and seafood, including pan-fried walleye. The impressive traditional mahogany and brass bar is worth a look even if you don't plan to imbibe. It features a massive number of single-malt scotches (scotch lovers, ask about the Scotch Club), an extensive wine list, and a beautifully lit back bar. The St. Paul Grill serves lunch and dinner daily and a popular and elegant brunch on Sunday.

350 Market St., St. Paul
651-224-7455
stpaulgrill.com

Top left: Apron-clad servers await diners at the St. Paul Grill. Photo by St. Paul Grill

Top right: The massive bar highlights a vast selection of single-malt scotch. Photo by St. Paul Grill

Above left: Scallops with couscous. Photo by St. Paul Grill

Above right: The St. Paul Grill is known in part as a great place for business lunches and dinners, but its location makes it a winner for special occasions and pre-theater meals too. Photo by St. Paul Grill

SALTY TART

Michelle Gayer is a multi-time James Beard nominee, and if you stop by Salty Tart—her little venue at Midtown Global Market—just once, you'll see why she is recognized as one of the best pastry chefs in the country. Even before you bite into one of the Tart's gorgeous cakes, pastries, breads, or tarts, stop to take in their mouthwatering beauty. They're so pretty it seems a shame to eat them, but, of course, you must.

Sweet, savory, crusty, frosted . . . Salty Tart bakes all these goodies using seasonal, local, and organic ingredients. Depending on the day, you'll find sweets, such as pastry cream-filled brioche, pearl-almond galette, apple streusel danish, and lovely fruit-filled tarts. Those with a yen for savory flavors should go for ham and cheese croissants, quiche, and savory turnovers. Breads include sourdough, crusty baguettes, and a rotating list of loaves, such as Minnesota wild wheat, jalapeño cheddar, and cinnamon raisin—all baked here in the four-hundred-square-foot bakery. It also serves sandwiches Monday through Friday. You can custom order cakes with a choice of filling and frosting. If you can't make it to the Midtown Global Market, you can order Salty Tart's cookies and famous coconut macaroons by the dozen online to be shipped to you.

920 E. Lake St., Minneapolis
612-874-9206
saltytart.com

Top right: The Salty Tart is known for its savory pastries, such as focaccia and scones.

Above left. Salty Tart owner and chef Michelle Gayer regularly receives awards and recognition from such organizations as the James Beard Foundation.

Above right: They make a mean cupcake at the Salty Tart; this one is surly—with Surly beer, that is.

SEA CHANGE

Seafood takes center stage at Sea Change, located at Minneapolis's famed Guthrie Theater. The raw bar is piled with oysters on the half shell, and starters include tuna carpaccio, octopus, abalone, and grilled shrimp. Paired with a glass of vino, they make ideal choices for a pre-theater nosh. The dinner menu highlights such entrées as trout, swordfish, tagliatelle pasta with smoked sturgeon and crème fraîche, and wonderful bouillabaisse. Sea Change is particularly proud that its fish come from sustainably harvested sources using environmentally responsible methods of gathering and farming seafood. Not a fish fan? They've got you covered with "Not Fish"—chicken, hanger steak, and crispy tofu.

The decor at this elegant eatery also evokes the ocean with watery colors and some furniture that was fashioned from windstorm-felled redwood trees. Even if you don't have theater tickets, drop by for lunch or dinner (and brunch on Vikings home game days) and take a tour of the Guthrie, which was designed by the Pritzker Prize-winning architect Jean Nouvel. Don't miss stepping out onto

Minneapolis has its roots here along the Mississippi riverfront, where timber and grain from around the Midwest came to market on the river and where St. Anthony Falls powered the flour mills of the Pillsbury family and others starting in the 1870s. It's home to the Mill City Museum and Mill Ruins Park, where visitors can trace the city's history, but do an about-face from the river and you'll see the latest and largest addition to the city's skyline—the ultra-modern U.S. Bank Stadium, home to the Minnesota Vikings.

Top left: Counter seating offers a view of the action and the raw bar at Sea Change. Photo by Sea Change Restaurant

Top right: Roasted beets with rye and walnuts. Photo by Sea Change Restaurant

Above left: Sea Change has an outdoor patio with a view of the Mississippi River, great for dining and pre-theater drinks. Photo by Sea Change Restaurant

Above center: Salmon terrine crème fraîche and moutarde violette with caraway crackers. Photo by Sea Change Restaurant

Above right: Ahi tuna with eggplant, fennel, olive, and orange. Photo by Sea Change Restaurant

the famous Endless Bridge that cantilevers out from the building to reveal a sensational view of the Mississippi riverfront, St. Anthony Falls, and the Stone Arch Bridge.

806 S. Second St., Minneapolis
612-225-6499
seachangempls.com

SPARKS

Sparks is a little gem of a bistro set in Minneapolis's Bryn Mawr neighborhood. With Sparks's success, the once tiny eatery has expanded but still retains its mellow, intimate feel, small enough to feel personal but big enough to offer a variety of food that is both creative and comforting. It's an especially popular place in the summer, when its big garage-style windows open onto the sidewalk patio.

The menu features such starters as meatballs, mussels, hummus, and warm olives. You'll find soup, salad, classic burgers, and gourmet sandwiches, such as the chorizo with roasted red peppers and chimichurri sauce. Larger plates include brick oven-roasted chicken, pot roast, and seared salmon. Relax here and watch workers toss and bake artisan pizzas in the wood-fired brick oven. Pizza versions include creative combos, such as the Meat Lovers with lamb merguez, fennel sausage, pepperoni, and mozzarella; Truffle and Egg, with braised kale and pecorino; and Verdura, with roasted onions, kalamata olives, roasted tomatoes, red peppers, arugula, and mozzarella. Choose from a nice selection of wine or local brews to accompany it all, and cap it with butterscotch panna cotta. Sparks is open daily for lunch and dinner.

230 Cedar Lake Rd. S., Minneapolis
612-259-8943
sparksminneapolis.com

Top right: Pizza dough ready for the tossing.

Above left: The mood at the Bryn Mawr eatery Sparks is friendly and laid-back.

Above right: Wood-fired margherita pizza.

SPOON AND STABLE

Spoon and Stable chef Gavin Kaysen has a reputation not only for his elegant cuisine and James Beard Award-winning restaurant in Minneapolis's trendy North Loop neighborhood but also for his collection of spoons—and how he obtains them.

The lure of spoons began for the Minnesota native when he was a twenty-one-year-old pastry chef in Lausanne, Switzerland. When he mastered how to make the perfect quenelle (an elegant oval scoop), he kept the spoon he was using as a memento. He continued that habit of spoon pilfering, though chefs and restaurants now give them to him as gifts. His collection inspired this restaurant's name, along with the fact that it's located in what was originally a horse stable built in 1906.

Kaysen says that for him spoons offer a tangible memory of an experience, whether it was a great meal, outstanding service, or a beautiful dining space. Spoon and Stable offers all three, striking just the right balance between no-nonsense heartland style and a staid elegance that fits this city well. That's why the restaurant has garnered raves from national food critics and locals alike.

Kaysen's cuisine melds hearty Midwestern food traditions with the fine French cooking style he honed while working in Europe and more recently as executive chef at Café Boulud in New York City. For example, you'll find Dorothy's Pot Roast: a homey favorite, yes, but it's served with pommes aligot, mushroom confit, carrots, and rosemary broth—quite unlike your mom's version. Pasta? Yes, but this dish consists of farro dumplings, goat goulash, crème fraîche, and paprika. Desserts offer a creative and satisfying mix of taste and texture. For instance, the black sesame sundae layers chocolate custard, butter brittle, and caramel.

If you reserve far enough ahead, you may be able to score a couple of seats at the counter next to the open kitchen, where you can watch chefs prepare your food with meticulous precision. Or, pull up a stool at the beautiful bar, where bartenders mix cocktail standards and newer concoctions and will even surprise you with a "bartender's choice" if you request. Check out Spoon and Stable for brunch and late-night ramen too.

Top left: Chef and owner Gavin Kaysen and executive pastry chef Diane Yang. Photo by Bonjwing Photography

Top right: Mushroom and egg salad. Photo by Bonjwing Photography

Above left: An elegant bar serves up creative craft cocktails. Photo by Bonjwing Photography

Above right: A venison entrée at Spoon and Stable. Photo by Bonjwing Photography

Kaysen and company have opened a new establishment, Bellecour, in Wayzata, a Minneapolis suburb (739 Lake Street). It offers a mix of classic French dishes with seasonal Midwestern ingredients and flavors.

211 N. First St., Minneapolis
612-224-9850
spoonandstable.com

SURLY DESTINATION BREWERY

If you're a craft beer fan, you've probably already heard of Surly beer, if not quaffed a few (or many more) of them. What you may not know is how Surly changed the face of craft brewing in Minnesota or that Surly's eats are now as distinguished as its award-winning beers.

Here's the quick Surly Nation story. Back in 2004–2005, an obsessed homebrewer and a local brewmaster combined to convert a north Minneapolis family-owned abrasives factory into a small brewery. In early 2006, Surly released its first public offering, a wildly hoppy IPA called Furious. Local, national, and international acclaim for Surly's brews quickly followed; in 2007 alone, Surly was named Best American Brewery by *Beer Advocate* magazine, and ratebeer.com named its Russian imperial stout, Surly Darkness, as the best American beer (ratebeer.com has also ranked Surly as one of the top 100 breweries globally for ten years running). In 2011, an "outpouring" of public support from Surly Nation caused the Minnesota legislature to enact the "Surly Bill," thus allowing medium-sized Minnesota brewers to sell beer and food at their breweries for the first time.

Today, Surly offers delicious food and beer at its Destination Brewery. In the cavernous, main-level Beer Hall and Restaurant, diners are treated to twenty to twenty-four of Surly's finest brews on tap plus a full menu. No ordinary pub food here; the Beer Hall features a wide range of specialty bar snacks, charcuteries and cheeses, burgers and sandwiches, barbecue, seafood, pasta, and more. Knowledgeable "beer-tenders" help pair the right beer with the right food. During warmer weather, the Beer Hall opens into an equally spacious and inviting beer garden with benches, tables, and toasty fire pits. Seating at the Beer Hall is first come, first served, and thirty–forty minute waits for a communal table are not uncommon, but order a beer and have fun while you wait.

Top right: Friendly servers help guests choose the right beer and match brews with food.

Above left: Surly offers top-notch casual food.

Above right: Surly's Beer Hall offers beer, great food, and a view of its brewing vats.

520 Malcolm Ave. SE, Minneapolis
763-999-4040
surlybrewing.com

THE BACHELOR FARMER

The Bachelor Farmer was one of the first restaurants to set up in the North Loop and was a leader in establishing the neighborhood as a dining and entertainment hot spot. The name is a play on references from Garrison Keillor's public radio show, *A Prairie Home Companion*, where in the town of Lake Wobegon Norwegian bachelor farmers lacked social skills but grew excellent wheat.

The Bachelor Farmer's ties to local agriculture aren't fictional, however. It has tight relationships with local farmers and purveyors to obtain the best and freshest produce, and it was a neighborhood pioneer in growing herbs and vegetables on its rooftop "farm," which was the first of its kind in Minneapolis. Those great ingredients go into fare that draws inspiration from the local Scandinavian heritage and cuisine but with a contemporary, northern Minnesota sensibility that has won many awards and critical acclaim. So, Ole and Lena of local humor would get the idea of serving toast for dinner but be surprised at the toppings that come along—e.g., fresh cow's milk cheese, pancetta-onion jam, toasted seeds, and honey. The menu changes daily, but expect such entrée items as duck breast with roasted carrots; swiss chard and pickled mustard greens; grilled and braised lamb; and beef leg with bok choy, crimini mushrooms, and chestnuts. Even stoic Norwegians and Swedes feel outgoing and

The North Loop is located in the Minneapolis Warehouse Historic District adjacent to downtown and is named after the trolley line circuit once there. The North Loop is Minneapolis's hippest and fastest-growing neighborhood. The industrial warehouses and factory buildings of its origins now house galleries, restaurants, bars, shops, and a growing amount of residential housing.

Top right: The Bachelor Farmer's signature pork meatballs, served with potato puree, lingonberry jam, and pickled cucumbers. Photo by the Bachelor Farmer

Above left: One of Marvel Bar's original cocktails, the Ladykiller, mixing gin, sochu, water, and rose wine. Photo by the Bachelor Farmer

Above right: The Bachelor Farmer Café serves toast, sandwiches, and salads for lunch and fabulous pastries and coffee all day. Photo by the Bachelor Farmer

chatty in the Bachelor Farmer's cheery, rustic farmhouse atmosphere, especially on Sundays when it serves a homey three-course Sunday supper with roasted chicken, seasonal sides, and dessert.

The Bachelor Farmer's adjacent sunny café is open for breakfast and lunch and serves lighter fare, such as soups, open-faced sandwiches, and mouthwatering pastries. The award-winning Marvel Bar downstairs at the Bachelor Farmer strikes a different mood, with a transition from the farmhouse to a chic speakeasy atmosphere that would surprise those bachelor farmers.

50 N. Second Ave., Minneapolis
612-206-3920
thebachelorfarmer.com

THE COMMODORE BAR AND RESTAURANT

"**D**ear Gatsby, where shall we dine tonight?"

"Daisy, my darling, you know there's only one place for us—the Commodore!"

Indeed, the Commodore, which was for a while the home of *The Great Gatsby*'s creator and St. Paul native F. Scott Fitzgerald and his wife, Zelda. Masterfully restored to its full Art Deco glory, the Commodore transports its guests back to the elegance, glamour, and carefree charm of the Jazz Age.

Built in 1920 as a residential hotel, the Commodore was the premier St. Paul destination for writers, celebrities, and other movers and shakers of the day, in part because of its Prohibition-era speakeasy, amply stocked by local bootleggers. Thanks to St. Paul's "O'Connor Rule," which sheltered visiting criminals from arrest (in exchange for a small fee), the Commodore was also a popular stopover for '20s and '30s era gangsters, including Al Capone, Ma Barker and family, and many others. After Prohibition ended in 1934, the Commodore opened its magnificent Art Deco bar and restaurant, designed by Werner Wittcamp, a designer for the Ziegfeld Follies and other memorable screen and stage sets, and modeled after a luxury ocean liner's lounge.

After a 1978 natural gas explosion devastated its interior, the hotel was repaired and converted into condominiums in 1983, but it took another thirty-two years for Wittcamp's iconic creation to be meticulously restored to its former grandeur. Today, the Commodore is again an Art Deco jewel, with gold leaf ceilings, glass chandeliers, tiled checkerboard floors, and beveled mirrors throughout its three intimate lounges and separate dining room. Other period touches abound, including dozens of black-and-white photographs of celebrities of the '30s and '40s, Deco lamps, furniture, objets d'art, and the Commodore's original 1930s stand-up bar.

Happily, the Commodore's food and drink are fitting complements to its historic prominence. Among the appetizers, the lobster deviled eggs, bacon-wrapped dates, and tartare creations are delightful

Top left: The Commodore's menu offers a primer on the Jazz Age.

Above left: F. Scott and Zelda Fitzgerald lived for a time in the Commodore.

Above right: The bar mixes appropriately named cocktails, such as the "Zelda" and "Evelyn's Elixir" (after John Dillinger's girlfriend).

accompaniments to one (or more) of the Commodore's signature cocktails, many named after some of St. Paul's more illustrious writers, artists, politicians, and gangsters of the era. Entrées are for the most part classic American dishes, including beef, pork, fowl, seafood, and vegetarian offerings. Both the spirits collection—intentionally featuring distillers located within a bootlegger's driving distance—and the wine list are extensive and superb.

The Commodore accepts reservations only for the dining room; the lounges are all first-come, first-served, but the same menu is available throughout. Parking is available in the Commodore's adjacent lot or on nearby streets.

79 Western Ave. N., St. Paul
651-330-5999
thecommodorebar.com

THE HAPPY GNOME

If you were a gnome residing in an award-winning restaurant serving up eighty-nine separate craft and imported beers on tap, more than 250 different whiskeys and terrific steaks, chops, burgers, sandwiches, and pub snacks, all in a casual, comfortable atmosphere—well, you'd be pretty happy too.

An annual fixture on *Draft* magazine's list of America's 100 Best Beer Bars, the Happy Gnome is a craft beer and whiskey lover's paradise. Most local craft brewers are represented, plus other acclaimed regional and national craft beers and a selection of high-quality imports. Seasonal brews abound, and the list of eighty-nine changes frequently, so the best way to find out what's on tap is to walk in the front door. Knowledgeable bartenders are on hand to educate and guide overwhelmed customers, and each month The Happy Gnome hosts a wildly popular "beer dinner," pairing a chosen brewer's offerings with delicious chef-selected food courses. The Happy Gnome's annual Firkin Fest puts sixty-plus firkins from Minnesota and across the country to tasting and popular vote, with the coveted Golden Firkin going to the winner. Its extraordinary selection of bourbons, ryes, and American, Canadian, Irish, and Scotch whiskies is among the best in the Twin Cities. For those preferring white or red adult beverages, the Happy Gnome also offers a selection of quality wines.

Lunch and dinner options are equally diverse and anything but typical bar food. The Happy Gnome sports everything from tasty pub favorites (e.g., broccoli and cheddar tater tots, BBQ wings, hot baked pretzels, and poutine), specialty pizzas, and mouthwatering burgers and sandwiches (including game, fowl, and veggie offerings) to grilled steaks and chops, beer-braised short ribs, and fresh seafood, all accompanied by imaginative side dishes. Delicious charcuterie and artisan cheese boards are great for sharing, and the dessert menu is stocked with unique house-made delights, including Surly beer-infused crème brulee, chocolate bread pudding with bourbon glaze, and almond and orange pot de crème. The Gnome Hot Brown, beer-braised pork belly hash, and enormous build-it-yourself Bloody Mary bar, among other items, are favorites among Sunday brunchers.

Left: This happy gnome greets guests.

Right: A beer and scotch lover's heaven.

The restaurant's cozy interior, in keeping with its name, is festooned with gnomes of every size, shape, color, and dress imaginable. During warmer months, guests may drink and dine on the Happy Gnome's lovely outdoor patio on a first-come, first-served basis. For inside dining, reservations are highly recommended. Ample parking is available adjacent to the building.

498 Selby Ave., St. Paul
651-287-2018
thehappygnome.com

THE HERBIVOROUS BUTCHER

Animals and vegans rejoice! A meat-free butcher may sound strange, but the Herbivorous Butcher offers meat-free meat and cheese-free cheese that's a hit with both vegans and "vegetarian aware" carnivores. Siblings Aubry and Kale Walch launched the Herbivorous Butcher in 2016, one of the first of its kind in the world. Aubry told the *New York Times*, "Our goal is to fool people into saving the planet."

This looks just like a traditional butcher shop, though decidedly more stylish and shiny clean without all the gooey, bloody stuff one sees in a meat market. As in an old-time establishment, "butchers" behind the counter wear paper hats and slice up your order. Shoppers who gaze into the meat case find offerings that include porterhouse steaks, filet mignon, brats, maple-glazed bacon, ribs and chops, chicken, and more, but instead of being grown in pastures, these mock meats are whipped up in the back, in small batches, and made with vital wheat gluten. Others, such as the pulled pork, are gluten free. No cows, sheep, or goats were milked in the making of Herbivorous cheese, either. Instead, surprisingly realistic sriracha cheddar, camembert, swiss, mozzarella, and pepper jack are created from veggies.

One of the keys to success at the Herbivorous Butcher is the taste. The shop takes a more flavorful, more culinary approach to making mock fare than many other artificial meat producers. The Italian sausage, for example, with sun-dried tomatoes, herbs, and spices, has a texture and flavor that would appeal to most serious meat lovers.

This isn't a restaurant, but you can order goodies, such as Italian cold cut or turkey dill-havarti sandwiches, a chimichurri and steak hoagie, and ready-made soups, to take away. While you're there, check out the other vegan gourmet products from local and national companies that line the shelves. You'll find kombucha, snack foods, and bee-free honey.

Top left: Siblings Aubry and Kale Walch, owners of the Herbivorous Butcher. Photo by the Herbivorous Butcher

Top right: A meat-free Italian sub sandwich. Photo by the Herbivorous Butcher

Above left: A selection of cheese-free cheese at the Herbivorous Butcher

Above right: A look at the "meat," featuring ribs, chops, bacon, and more. Photo by the Herbivorous Butcher

If you can't make it into the shop, the Herbivorous Butcher also offers an online list of products to order. These include kits to make dinners for special occasions, such as Valentine's Day; pizza; and a vegan starter kit with its most popular items, meal plans, and recipes and meat-free meat for twenty-four meals and six snacks.

507 First Ave. NE, Minneapolis
612-208-0992
theherbivorousbutcher.com

THE KENWOOD

Kenwood isn't your average neighborhood—or restaurant. Food at the Kenwood eatery is simple enough to bring the children but subtle and sophisticated enough to satisfy food lovers who seek interesting culinary twists, perfect presentation, and friendly service.

Brunch crab cakes, for example, are as pretty as they are tasty, with piquillo pepper, swiss chard, poached eggs, and hollandaise. Mixed greens go beyond the typical "house salad," with citrus, fennel, and feta, and those crispy things on top are parsnips. Even the burgers have an international flair, with tomato aioli on a brioche bun, and The Kenwood burger adds pork belly, gruyere, and a fried egg. Kenwood entrées include venison loin, short ribs, wild boar pappardelle, and other options that change weekly and with the seasons—simple but elegant. The decor has a subtle old-money look,

Kenwood is considered part of the Calhoun Isles area adjacent to Minneapolis's famous Chain of Lakes. It's one of the city's most affluent neighborhoods and dates back to the 1800s, making it a lovely place to stroll and gaze at its historic mansions. Look for the home of Kenwood's most famous fictional resident, Mary Richards of the *Mary Tyler Moore Show*, at 2104 Kenwood Parkway, and be sure to visit author Louise Erdrich's bookstore, Birchbark Books, right next door to the Kenwood restaurant. The parkland surrounding Lake of the Isles and Lake Calhoun offers great opportunities for walking, biking, sailing, and paddling, too.

Top right: The Kenwood's cozy dining room is decorated with oil paintings and wood paneling.

Above left: The Kenwood's casual feel makes it perfect for a meal and a walk around the neighborhood.

Above right: Crab cakes with colorful pepper sauce, swiss chard, and poached eggs.

with pine paneling, a long banquette running the length of one wall, plaid wallpaper, and paintings of hunting dogs and old farm scenes. Vintage photos give a feel for the neighborhood's early days.

Combine a visit to this restaurant with a tour of one of Minneapolis's loveliest neighborhoods. You'll fall in love with Kenwood—the neighborhood and the eatery. Open all day serving breakfast, brunch, snacks, and dinner.

2115 W. Twenty-First St., Minneapolis
612-377-3695
thekenwoodrestaurant.com

THE LEXINGTON

To see St. Paulites in their native habitat, head for the Lexington. "The Lex," as it's more commonly and fondly known, first opened its doors in 1935. For generations, its beautiful wood-paneled dining rooms were the place for St. Paul dignitaries, politicos, celebs, and families celebrating special occasions to dine. It was a classic supper club of its era, with steaks, chops, and a beloved version of pot pie. Yet the Lex grew worn, changed hands several times, closed, and was nearly consigned to the history of restaurants past. But in 2017, after a multimillion-dollar renovation, the Lex reopened to rave reviews. The wood has been refinished and chandeliers shined (with a complete building rehab behind the scenes), the decor burnished with a touch of modernity, and everything smacks of elegance.

Now this establishment walks a fine line between its tradition and its future, striving for a menu that keeps the old guard happy but current and exciting enough to lure new generations Fortunately, the new crew has experience aplenty to do the job. Executive Chef Jack Riebela James Beard Award nominee for best chef, grew up in St. Paul and ate pot pie at the Lex as a child.

General Manager Sara Luoma describes the new Lex as "an elevated supper club." Two bars, the Martini Bar and the Williamsburg Room, with its plush couches and leather chairs and stained-glass windows, feature friendly bartenders who mix classic cocktails, such as old-style martinis and old fashioneds, a special Punch du Lex, and local brews and wine. The bar menu features garlic parsley fries with truffle aioli, oysters on the half shell, burgers with a bit of kimchi and sweet mayo, fried chicken sliders, and, yes, pot pie. On the dinner menu, appetizers include updated versions of beef tartare (with salted mango), mushroom cap escargot, and liver and onions. A Lex Salad contains the iceberg lettuce of yore but with smoky olives and marinated tomatoes. You'll find steaks and chops on the menu, the specialty steak Diane, and "Whitefish à la Gorbachev" as it was prepared when Soviet leader Mikhail Gorbachev visited the Lex in the 1980s. Pastas include duck and foie meatballs in stroganoff and a nod to vegetarians with cauliflower cappellacci with smoked almonds, raisins, and capers.

Top right: The updated house salad at the Lex.

Above left: The back bar at this newly remodeled St. Paul landmark.

Above right: Mixing cocktails at the Lexington's Martini Bar.

The Williamsburg Room also takes on the air of a true cocktail lounge Thursday through Saturday with live jazz music from 6:00 p.m. to 9:30 p.m. Then the Williamsburg Vinyl Club takes over, with a rotating list of DJs handling the music. A rooftop patio opens in summer with views of some of the most beautiful neighborhoods around. The Lex draws much of its clientele from the neighborhood, but as word spreads, expect folks even from Minneapolis to cross the river, maybe dress up a little, and join the natives.

1096 Grand Ave., St. Paul
651-289-4990
thelexmn.com

THE SIOUX CHEF

You may not have experienced Native American cuisine, given that there are just a handful of eateries devoted to that concept across the country. Yet, in the world of trendy eateries offering "slow, organic, and natural" food, cuisine from America's first peoples has them all beat. Chef Sean Sherman and his crew are working to bring precolonial food to the forefront, serving it at catered events and from their Tatanka Truck, which cruises the Twin Cities in summer. He uses ingredients true to Dakota and Ojibwe tradition, including heirloom corn, beans, and squash; wild rice; berries; bergamot; rose hips; and wild onions. For protein, Sioux Chef dishes incorporate local lake fish, duck, goose, quail, and game meats, such as venison, bison, rabbit, and turkey. Look for the Sioux Chef restaurant, expected to open at the end of 2017.

612-486-2433
tatankatruck.com
sioux-chef.com

Wild rice, known as manoomin in Ojibwe, is the Minnesota state grain and is found in eateries and at family dinners all around the Twin Cities. It's a staple of fashionable gourmet cooks but is even more important in the daily lives of Ojibwe and other Native American peoples, who use the rice in ceremonies and feasts and rely on it as an important source of income.

Top right: Healthy and beautiful, the bison wild rice bowl combines cedar-braised bison, maple-roasted veggies, greens, and toasted seeds. Photo by the Sioux Chef

Above left: Native Americans harvest wild rice from local lakes using sticks to beat the seeds into the canoe. Photo by Minnesota Department of Natural Resources

Above right: The folks at The Sioux Chef and their Tatanka Truck food truck utilize ingredients such as walleye and wild rice to showcase the food of indigenous Americans. Photo by the Sioux Chef

TINY DINER

Don't let the name confuse you. Tiny Diner isn't all that tiny, in size or ambition. This laid-back neighborhood eatery makes its homey diner food with a major emphasis on fresh, locally raised ingredients. Hey, you can't get more local than herbs and veggies raised in the garden by the patio or from Tiny Diner's nearby urban patch, Tiny Farm. It also aims to create dishes with the same careful preparation one finds in bigger, fancier places.

Tiny Diner's menu is fairly simple and changes each month to include traditional diner-type items in the style of a different city across the US. Breakfast and lunch merge with egg dishes. Burritos to quiche are served along with salads and sandwiches, including the spinach and walnut burger, and cater to meat lovers and vegetarians alike. Reliable standards include salads, such as the kale salad with brussels sprouts, pistachios, and lemon vinaigrette; chicken pot pie that's more like chicken and biscuits, topped with an egg; and pot roast with cheesy corn grits, broccoli, and guajillo (pepper) jus. Tiny Diner's drink menu offers an excellent selection of local brews, cocktails, and wine. The casual atmosphere—and such foods as the mac and cheese—make this an easy place to bring children.

You can detect the outlines of the gas station that used to stand on the Tiny Diner site, but how things have changed! Counters that probably once sold oil and auto parts now serve customers. In summer, Tiny Diner becomes a tiny bit of country in the city because the entire site was redesigned using permaculture concepts. For example, fruit trees and other plants now grow around the building, and rainwater runoff waters the plants. Solar panels that supply much of the restaurant's energy create a roof over the patio area where motorists once pumped their gas, and honey bees inhabit hives on the roof. That all fits with Tiny Diner's goal not only to fill tummies with great food but also to create community, to inspire urban gardeners, and to demonstrate techniques that assist the environment.

Top left: Tiny Diner's roasted vegetable sandwich: squash, eggplant, red onion, preserved tomato, and chevre. Photo by Eric Melzer

Top right: Diners now enjoy an outdoor patio where motorists once pumped gas. The roof is made of solar panels. Photo by Eric Melzer

Above left: Tiny Diner's colorful counter area doesn't look like a gas station anymore. Photo by Eric Melzer

Above right: Not your average diner fare—smoked turkey liver mousse with pickled berries and shaved radish on caraway toast. Photo by Eric Melzer

Tiny Diner serves breakfast, lunch, and dinner as well as a "tiny" four-dollar happy hour Monday through Friday from 3:00 p.m. to 6:00 p.m. and brunch on weekends. On Thursday evenings in summer, a farmers' market pops up on the property, where neighbors and diners find local produce, artisan bread, fresh eggs, live music, and more.

1024 E. Thirty-Eighth St., Minneapolis
612-767-3322
tinydiner.com

TONGUE IN CHEEK

Combining a passion for sustainable food and drink with epicurean excellence in a casual, light-hearted atmosphere catering to carnivores and herbivores alike, Tongue in Cheek is widely recognized as one of St. Paul's go-to restaurants and a linchpin of the East Side's blooming culinary scene.

Its wildly inventive fare comes in three distinct serving styles. Five "teasers"—bite-sized dollops of creativity—are mini masterpieces of flavor, color, and texture. One example is the "Winter Blues," a soup spoon–sized explosion of concentrated blueberry sphere, basil oil, blue cheese, sea salt, and toffee nuts. Delicious small plates, easily divisible among two to three diners, include steamed barbecue pork buns, beef tartare with capers and pine nuts, pan-seared scallops with chorizo in a sweet potato puree, and ricotta gnocchi with arugula pesto and parmesan cheese. Entrée-sized large plates range from pork belly and grits; a bacon, egg, and pork belly ramen; and a sensational grass-fed cheeseburger to the "Daily Vegasm," the chef's vegan surprise. Note that menu items and ingredients vary with the season, availability, and freshness. Tongue in Cheek also offers separate seven-course tasting menus for vegans and everyone else, with or without paired libations, and brunch Wednesday through Sunday.

Specialty cocktails, equally imaginative, are ranked by taste—sweet, spicy, salty, bitter, sour, and umami. Indecisive drinkers can order a sampling of all six, add on a flight of all five teasers, and send every taste bud on the tongue into culinary ecstacy. Tongue in Cheek also features a wide range of bourbons and ryes; red, white, and sparkling wines; local and regional craft bottled beers; and a popular 4:00–7:00 p.m. daily happy hour.

Uniquely committed to sustainability, Tongue in Cheek pledges that every animal product it serves, including meat, eggs, and dairy, comes from animals raised or caught in a humane and sustainable manner. It also carefully reviews its produce, beer, and wine suppliers' sustainability practices before buying from them, and wherever possible everything is locally sourced. Also unique is Tongue in Cheek's bohemian vibe; large, colorful modern art oils are displayed throughout, and antique mirrors of every size and shape hang behind

Top right: Fried green tomatoes with burrata cheese. Photo by Tongue in Cheek

Above left: Tongue in Cheek's Naughty Scotty cocktail. Photo by Tongue in Cheek

Above right: Tongue in Cheek's East Fried Pride teaser—pork belly with mango and peanut. Photo by Tongue in Cheek

and around the bar. The net result—a socially conscious yet lively and unpretentious restaurant determined not to take itself too seriously.

Tongue in Cheek is closed on Mondays. Reservations are accepted and highly recommended on weekends. A small parking lot lies immediately behind the restaurant; street and neighborhood parking are also available.

989 Payne Ave., St. Paul
651-888-6148
tongueincheek.biz

TORI RAMEN

❝We have plenty of napkins," says one server at Tori Ramen. That's good, because there's really no way to eat ramen, with its flipping and splattering noodles, broth, veggies, and meat, but to inhale the fragrance and start slurping. Despite the number of Twin Cities eateries serving ramen and pho, the folks at Tori Ramen set out to stand out in the world of broth and noodles. That's all they serve, so they do it well, but there's an added twist. Most ramen broth is made with pork, but the broth at Tori Ramen comes from fowl (chicken or duck) or vegetables, thus opening the ramen to people from a larger number of cultural traditions. You'll want to work your way through the menu from the heaviest—the Bali Bali with ground chicken is the most hearty—down to lighter versions, such as the Salted Duck and Me So What?, and you can watch them make it in the open kitchen. Drinks include beer, wine, kombucha, and rotating variations of fruit-filled and very refreshing tasting vinegar.

Tori Ramen offers a stylish atmosphere with rustic wood, black walls, and colorful banners that say the restaurant's name in Chinese, Japanese, and Korean. Open for lunch and dinner Wednesday through Sunday.

161 Victoria St. N., St. Paul
651-340-4955
toriramen.com

Left: Banners written in Chinese, Japanese, and Korean drape the walls at Tori Ramen.

Right: Salted duck ramen. Dishes at Tori Ramen are made without the typical pork broth.

TRAVAIL KITCHEN AND AMUSEMENTS

Imagine you're at the theater watching a Cirque du Soleil performance . . . except you're not in the audience but up on stage with the performers . . . and the performers aren't acrobats but master chefs preparing masterpieces of culinary art. That, in a nutshell, is an evening at Travail—a high-energy tour de force of molecular gastronomy and one of the most unique dining experiences in the Twin Cities.

Here are the basics. Wednesday through Saturday evenings, Travail features a prix fixe chef's tasting menu numbering fifteen to twenty or more rapid-fire "courses," each an exquisite one-to-two-bite melding of extraordinary flavors, textures, and colors. À la carte craft beer, wine, and custom cocktails are available, and with notice Travail can accommodate diners' vegetarian/vegan preferences or food allergies. Courses are served on or in plates, spoons, sticks, skewers, or bowls; caught out of the air; suspended at mouth level; or dolloped on the back of one's hand. Guests sit at communal tables of eight, each manned by four mad scientists/chefs who concoct and meticulously explain each individual course. Travail's kitchen, serving stations, and guest tables all inhabit the same open environment; indeed, some courses are cooked or frozen (yes, liquid nitrogen) tableside, and guests are led into the kitchen to enjoy others. The open-joisted ceiling hosts a menagerie of stuffed animals and cartoon superheroes staring at the goings-on below, and Travail's waggish "Sexy Chef Calendar" adds to the collective whimsy and revelry.

But make no mistake. Travail's chefs are serious about their food. Consider, for instance, a steamed dumpling filled with root vegetable and pork cheek ragu, drizzled in a Fresno chili-and-vinegar sauce and accompanied by a steamed mussel, mascarpone cheese, chives, and microgreens. Or a romaine, mizuna, rutabaga, celery, and celery root salad wrapped in a slice of dry-aged, New York steak carpaccio and topped with a black truffle/Chartreuse demi-glace and shaved fresh horseradish. Or salmon tartare and faux caviar (tapioca pearls

Top left: The Travail team often assembles dishes at your table. Photo by Courtney Perry

Top right: Travail cultivates a casual, whimsical atmosphere. Photo by Courtney Perry

Above left: The chefs at Travail are also the entertainment. Photo by Courtney Perry

Above right: Eat your peas! They've never looked or tasted so great. Photo by Courtney Perry

in squid ink) with mini garlic chips, a ginger/jalapeno sauce, and fresh wasabi. Each of these is a single course, meticulously prepared and stylishly presented. Add another twelve to eighteen equally elaborate amuse-bouche, vegetable, seafood, fowl, meat, and dessert courses, and it's no wonder that Travail is a favorite of serious gastronomes from across the country.

Advance ticketing for Travail through its website is a virtual necessity, and weekend reservations in particular sell out weeks in advance. Be sure to check in on Travail-related cateries—the adjacent Rookery and Pig Ate My Pizza, just down the street.

4124 W. Broadway Ave.
Robbinsdale, MN 55422
763-535-1131
travailkitchen.com

TULLIBEE

Casual but cool, the "up north chic" ethos of the boutique Hewing Hotel fits perfectly into its trendy North Loop neighborhood. The Hewing's lovely bar and restaurant, Tullibee, looks like a glitzy northern lodge. It's atmosphere melds the rough lumberjack-hewn beams and a feel of Minnesota's northern woods with the steel and stone and exposed brick of its urban warehouse location. Huge windows looking onto the street corner feel wide open to the outside and connect with the rich history of the city.

The food connects too. Tullibee is named after a type of small whitefish, also known as cisco, that is found in the cold lakes of the North. As that name hints, everything at Tullibee is locally grown and made, from the food right down to the drink cozys made at Faribault Woolen Mill that cover hot drinks like tiny wool blankets.

You can watch the cooks at work in Tullibee's wide-open kitchen, complete with wood-burning grill and oven and slabs of hanging meat. The ever-changing and minimalist menu gives a nod to the region's Nordic heritage and the foods that have traditionally been part of Minnesota life. For example, for lunch, you may find oh-so-Minnesotan chicken and wild rice soup and traditional Scandinavian smorrebrod, an open-faced sandwich with gravlax, red onion, potted cheese, and pickled cucumber. Yet the menu doesn't fit easily under one label, and the whole Nordic concept serves mostly as a springboard for culinary creativity. Tullibee serves Scandinavian dishes, such as lefse—a potato pancake that looks like a tortilla—but tops it with fingerlime, radishes, and rabbit belly. There are meatballs, yes, but they're in soup and made of duck. Curry and other decidedly un-Scandinavian spices weave into many dishes, and the artful presentation looks more delicate and Asian than husky and North Woods. Dinner favorites include duck with a sauce of grilled bones, a changing list of fish, and perfectly grilled beef, and don't miss the french fries cooked to crisp perfection in duck fat.

Tullibee serves breakfast, lunch, and dinner. Keep an eye out for the Hewing's hotel parties and special events that will open the rooftop bar to the general public, offering a chance to see the twinkling cityscape come to life.

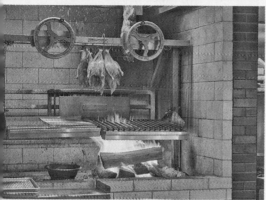

Top left: Food at Tullibee reflects Minnesota's north woods heritage. Photo by Tullibee

Top right: Tullibee's bar, with the wooden deer head, is a favorite gathering place. Photo by Tullibee

Above left: Food is roasted over an open flame. Photo by Tullibee

Above right: Tullibee's dining room features Nordic design and is open to the kitchen. Photo by Tullibee

300 Washington Ave., Minneapolis
866-501-3300
hewinghotel.com/tullibee-restaurant

UNITED NOODLES
AND UNIDELI

Featured on the Food Network's *Diners, Drive-Ins and Dives,*
Unideli is a small, hugely popular Asian food counter tucked away
in the center of United Noodles, Minnesota's largest Asian grocery
store. A cult favorite among Twin Cities ramen aficionados, Unideli's
signature ramen, called Dramen, is a delectable combination of
hybrid broth, ramen noodles, long strips of pork belly, crunchy
bamboo shoots, caramelized onions, black garlic oil, leeks, and soy
egg, topped with crushed peanuts. Other popular ramens include
the fiery Tantanmen (spicy sesame broth with ground pork, noodles,
bok choy, enoki mushrooms, leeks, peanuts, chili flakes, Thai chilis,
Sichuan peppercorns, and a slow-poached egg), and Tonkotsu (pork,
noodles, bean sprouts, bok choy, leeks, sesame, soy egg, and red

After the fall of Saigon in 1975, hundreds of thousands of
Vietnamese, Hmong, and Cambodians who had been loyal
to America during the war, now fearful for their lives, fled to
refugee camps in Thailand. Thanks to more than a thousand
sponsoring Minnesota churches, assisted by dozens of aid
groups and local, state, and national governmental agencies,
tens of thousands of those migrants emigrated to Minnesota.
Today, more than seventy thousand ethnic Hmong alone
call Minneapolis-St. Paul home–the largest concentration of
urban Hmong in the world–and contribute significantly to
the Twin Cities' economy as physicians, lawyers, grocers, car
dealers, bankers, restaurateurs, hoteliers, artists, and more.

Left: Dramen at Unideli has sliced pork belly, Asian greens, noodles, peanuts, and chili flakes. A combination of chicken and pork broths adds to the richness. Photo by United Noodles

Right: A snack sampler of Spam Musabi, Takoyaki, and the Korean wings. Photo by United Noodles

pepper bomb). These and other imaginative ramens led the Daily Meal to rank Unideli as one of America's 25 Best Ramen Shops in 2014. Unideli also serves up to-die-for Chinese barbecued pork, authentic Japanese curried chicken and katsu, Korean double-fried chicken wings, and other Asian small plates and specialties.

The Hmong community has become a potent political force, as well, electing Hmong-American politicians to the Minnesota House and Senate, Minneapolis and St. Paul city councils, and other local offices.

While you're there, be sure to wander through United Noodles and its mind-blowing selection of Chinese, Japanese, Korean, Vietnamese, and other Asian grocery products. In-the-know chefs and foodies flock here to find fresh produce; Asian meats and seafood; and sauces, spices, noodles, and pantry items available nowhere else in the Twin Cities. United Noodles also holds annual special events celebrating the Lunar New Year; the Great United Noodles Easter Egg Hunt; the Autumn Luau; and the ethnic Chinese, Japanese, and Korean holidays. Ample parking adjoins the store.

2015 E. Twenty-Fourth St., Minneapolis
612-721-6677
unitednoodles.com

Opposite page: Lucky Cat hints at good luck for shoppers at United Noodles. Photo by United Noodles

VICTOR'S 1959 CAFÉ

Ricky Ricardo would feel right at home in Minneapolis's quirky little piece of Cuba, Victor's 1959 café. He'd probably order a big plate of picadillo and a mug of café Cubano. Then he'd write his name somewhere on the wall amidst other customers' graffiti that is scrawled on every square inch of the place, even the ceiling.

The Cuban Revolution took place in 1959, and one of the café's original owners, Victor Valens, hailed from Cuba—hence the name. This eye-catching tropically colored joint was originally a gas station, and it sits at one of the best intersections for food in Minneapolis, with Rincón 38 and Grand Café on the opposite corners.

The food is as colorful as the decor and billed as "revolutionary Cuban cooking." For breakfast, you'll find such items as an array of pancakes; Eggs Havana, served with black beans, creole sauce, and yuca frita, akin to fried potatoes; and more "American" eggs and french toast. For lunch, try a traditional Cuban sandwich or a café specialty, picadillo, with sautéed ground beef, red and green peppers, potatoes, Spanish green olives, capers, and raisins with a creole sauce. For dinner, Victor's naturally offers paella. Victor's food may inspire you to get out your conga drum and sing "Babalú."

3756 Grand Ave. S., Minneapolis
612-827-8948
victors1959cafe.com

Top: The name 1959 Café is a nod to the date of the Cuban Revolution.

Above left: A man-sized Cuban sandwich and black bean veggie soup.

Above right: A colorful plate of picadillo, a Victor's specialty.

VICTORY 44

Victory 44's heroic-sounding name (after the surrounding Victory neighborhood in the northwesternmost corner of Minneapolis) doesn't match its simple white exterior. Inside, with its rough wood floors and sports on the TVs over the bar, it resembles a typical neighborhood watering hole, which it is, but it's also a high-end gastropub that attracts folks from a much wider area with its casual but sophisticated fare. Victory 44 lists its small and changing menu on chalkboards around the restaurant. Each item is prepared with a gourmet flourish. The humbly named Perfect Burger is a bacon lover's delight with bits of bacon in the burger and cheese and bacon on top, and it arrives with bacon fries too. You'll find Devils on Horseback, bacon-wrapped dates in blue cheese sauce; and chicken and rice with fried chicken, buttered rice, peanuts, pickled gold

This neighborhood grew up in the 1920s and '30s surrounding a lovely tree-lined parkway, Victory Memorial Drive. Completed in 1921, the parkway was dedicated to the memory of Hennepin County soldiers and nurses who died in World War I. More recently, the area was designated a state historic district honoring all county soldiers who lost their lives in war. Though dedicated to the past, there's plenty of life here now. The parkway is part of the Grand Rounds Scenic Byway, and the expansive Victory Park adjacent to the parkway offers bike and running paths, making Victory another great Minneapolis neighborhood to explore for both dining and recreation.

Top: Artful desserts at Victory 44 add to its reputation as a high-end gastropub.

Above left: Chicken and rice with raisins and capers.

Above right: Victory 44's bacon-graced Perfect Burger.

raisins, capers, brown butter, and herbs. Pork schnitzel comes with honey-glazed peaches, charred onions, arugula, and goat cheese, and the artful desserts match those of higher-end eateries. Not surprisingly, it has a great selection of local brews, and servers happily suggest the best beer to pair with your food.

(Also look for Victory 44 chef Erick Harcey's other restaurant, the Scandinavian-focused Upton 43, in Minneapolis's Linden Hills neighborhood.)

2203 N. Forty-Fourth Ave., Minneapolis
612-588-2228
victory-44.com

VOLSTEAD'S EMPORIUM

Cranky Minnesota Congressman Andrew Volstead helped author the 18th Amendment to the Constitution that banned the sale of alcohol in the US from 1920 to 1933. Today's namesake, Volstead's Emporium, operates just like the Prohibition-era speakeasys that quickly sprouted up to serve the many citizens who continued to imbibe despite the law. They were secret "underground" establishments promising alcohol and entertainment away from the eyes of the law, all promoted by whispers and word of mouth. Nowadays, social media spreads the news, and judging by the lines outside Volstead's on the weekend, the word is out.

You'll perhaps feel akin to the Lost Generation of the 1920s as you search for Volstead's location just west of Lyndale Avenue on Lake Street. Despite the address, it's not really on Lake but in the back of the building, so walk through the alley between two buildings, veer left past the dumpsters, and look for the door with the red light over it. Knock and, when the slit in the door opens, tell the eyes looking out at you a password of your choosing to gain admission. The trek is worth it when the door opens downstairs and you're transported back to the Jazz Age. Period woodwork and a great many other fixtures have been reclaimed from other sites and fitted into this space so skillfully that any flapper would be fooled. There's a beautiful bar circa 1909 and several rooms outfitted with Victorian furniture and memorabilia. Guests access private dining rooms by an antique phone booth or a swinging fireplace facade. In the velvet-curtained booths, servers deliver food and drinks through mirrors in the wall that open and close.

Volstead's features vintage cocktails like those mixed during the Prohibition era, e.g., planters punch, old fashioneds, and the Lion's Tail with bourbon and lime. It shakes up other cocktails and offers an impressive bourbon selection, beer, and wine too. Still, it's not

Pssst. They're serving food and booze at Volstead's Emporium, but keep it under your hat.

194

Top left: Entering Volstead's is like stepping into a Jazz Age speakeasy. Photo by Volstead's Emporium

Top right: The Victorian bar at Volstead's was salvaged from an historic building. Photo by Volstead's Emporium

Above left: Diners enter this private dining room through an antique phone booth. Photo by Volstead's Emporium

Above right: In velvet-draped booths, food and cocktails arrive through the wall. Photo by Volstead's Emporium

all about drinking. Volstead's food menu changes quarterly. You'll find such items as mussels, charcuterie plates, pasta, burgers (veggie and meat), steelhead salmon, salads, and more to fuel your Jazz Age experience. There's often live music, from hot club to gypsy jazz–style bands reminiscent of the era.

Good luck finding Volstead's. If you do, consider yourself part of the in-crowd, and get ready for a good time.

711 Lake St., Minneapolis
find it on Facebook

W. A. FROST AND COMPANY

It's difficult to decide what's better at W. A. Frost ... the atmosphere or the food. It's set in one of St. Paul's most beautiful neighborhoods, Cathedral Hill, and the restaurant is located in the Dacotah Building, which was erected in 1889 and is on the National Register of Historic Places. W. A. Frost's Pharmacy, a tenant in this building in the early 1900s, inspired the eatery's name, and the pharmacy surely counted such folks as F. Scott Fitzgerald among its customers.

Frost's special lure changes with the season, as does its menu. In winter, you'll find a warm and romantic Victorian atmosphere, so romantic, in fact, that it's the frequent backdrop for wedding proposals. Here diners cozy up in the dining room, with its brick walls, oriental rugs, and original oil paintings and fireplaces. Or they gather in the historic bar, furnished with period furnishings and fixtures salvaged from buildings in the region.

But you can't eat atmosphere. Fortunately, W. A. Frost's menu isn't about to be overshadowed by all that historic decor. It offers a lengthy "something for everyone" list of American cuisine that changes with the seasons and emphasizes local ingredients. One highlight of eating at Frost's is shareability. For example, "plates to share" include mussels, ribs, and beef skewers that are great for groups to pass around. Ditto for the artisan cheese plates available

St. Paul's lumber and railroad barons and local politicians built their mansions here, and Cathedral Hill remains one of the city's loveliest neighborhoods. It's a great place for a walking tour to see the mansions and the place where F. Scott Fitzgerald was born (481 Laurel Avenue) and lived in a house that he famously described as "a house below the average on a street above the average."

Top right: The patio at W. A. Frost is a summertime favorite of Twin Citians. Photo by W. A. Frost

Above left: W. A. Frost's Victorian bar.

Above right: W. A. Frost is located in the Dacotah Building, which was built in 1889 and is on the National Register of Historic Places. Photo by W. A. Frost

with one, three, or five cheeses. You'll find burgers and spiced shrimp wraps, as well as sophisticated entrées (in "micro" and standard quantities), such as braised lamb shanks, pan-roasted whitefish, and penne pasta with rosemary and gorgonzola cream sauce. It also has a huge and award-winning wine list. Truly ambitious diners may select the chef's tasting menu for a tour of the menu and optional wine pairings.

W. A. Frost shines brightest when warm weather arrives. That's when Twin Citians shed their down coats and mad bomber hats and head outdoors to dine in droves. The patio's setting, with brick, huge trees, lush greenery, and twinkle lights, makes this a top spot for al fresco dining. W. A. Frost is one reason we wish summer lasted a lot longer. Open for lunch, dinner, and Saturday/Sunday brunch and happy hour, and it has many rooms available for private dining.

374 Selby Ave., St. Paul
651-224-5715
wafrost.com

WORLD STREET KITCHEN

Few eateries make the quantum leap from downtown food truck to one of *Bon Appetit*'s national Top 50 new restaurants, but with *Iron Chef* veteran and James Beard-nominated Sameh Wadi at the culinary helm, World Street Kitchen imports the tastes, smells, and textures of delectable global street cuisine into a casual, fun, Lyn-Lake Minneapolis setting.

In the mood for Asian? Try one of WSK's terrific "Yum Yum" rice bowls, filled with Korean BBQ short ribs and house-made kimchi, caramelized lamb belly and daikon, or lemongrass meatballs, each swathed in Chef Wadi's killer "secret sauce." Up for Middle Eastern? There's the amazing Moroccan fried chicken-on-a biscuit sandwich, the sweet onion-stuffed falafel burger, or grilled pita with hummus and smoked feta. Latin? You'll love the Mexican steak sandwich, with avocado, chipotle adobo, chihuahua cheese, and a fried egg. If you're in a multicultural mood, check out the red curry chicken burrito or beef shawarma tacos. Thirsty global explorers can rehydrate from a selection of tap and bottled beers, wines by the glass and bottle, and wine cocktails.

A favorite of urban hipsters, busy professionals, parents with young children, and everyone in between, WSK does not take reservations. Parking is available in an adjoining lot or on area streets.

2743 Lyndale Ave. S., Minneapolis
612-424-8855
eatwsk.com

Left: World Street Kitchen got its start as a food truck but has been acclaimed a top restaurant nationally.

Right: World Street Kitchen draws on many cultures to create surprising and satisfying flavor combinations.

YOUNG JONI

Just what, exactly, is Young Joni? Is it a stunningly designed, sumptuous eatery that also tosses some of the best pizzas in the Twin Cities? Or is it a pizza joint that also features an array of non-pie dishes and craft cocktails? It's both, and then some—"the restaurant of the future," as the *Star Tribune* proclaimed in 2017, and one of Nordeast's hottest dining spots.

Young Joni is an offshoot of James Beard-nominated Ann Kim's Pizzeria Lola, South Minneapolis's award-winning pizza parlor, and several of Kim's acclaimed pies, including her Korean BBQ pizza, have migrated north to Young Joni. But new pizza creations abound, including the decadent La Parisienne (prosciutto, gruyere, ricotta, brown butter, caramelized onions, and arugula); the Basque (chorizo, mozzarella and goat cheeses, piquillo pepper, red onions, olives, and preserved lemon); and Umami Mama (gourmet mushrooms, Taleggio and fontina cheeses, truffle oil, and nori). All incorporate perfect crusts—crispy outside, chewy inside—and are baked in Young Joni's enormous copper wood-fired pizza oven.

But there's a lot more to Young Joni than delicious pizza—in particular, a bevy of wonderfully creative, globally inspired small plates. Consider, for instance, the signature bibim grain salad, combining Job's tears and farro grains with brussels sprouts, zucchini, tare mushrooms, pickled vegetables, purple daikon, nori, mixed seeds, a poached egg, and gochujang (red Korean chili paste) vinaigrette, all beautifully presented. Other favorites, to name a few, include gently grilled kale and treviso (Italian radicchio) salads, Moroccan cauliflower with grilled shishito peppers, grilled blue prawns in a red chili fish sauce, and meatballs with kimchi and oxtail sugo. The daily seafood selection—often a whole fish, salt-encrusted and baked—is a treat for the whole table. Foodie heaven? You bet.

Young Joni is also an architectural gem. The dining room is spacious yet surprisingly cozy, thanks to rough-hewn pine beams and columns, a dropped dining room ceiling, and shelf after shelf of bric-a-brac—chic and comfy, modern and homey, all at the same

Top right: Young Joni has a rustic, wide-open atmosphere.

Above left: Ann Kim of Young Joni and Pizzeria Lola. Photo by Eliesa Johnson

Above right: Selections large and small—grilled blue prawns in a red chili fish sauce, meatballs with kimchi and oxtail sugo, and whole roasted fish—make great opportunities to taste and share. Photo by Eliesa Johnson

time. Communal dining tables near the elongated main bar add to the sensation of warmth and comfort. Not to be missed is Young Joni's secret bar, outside and down the alley from the restaurant. The dimly lit speakeasy features jazz, blues, and R&B played on a reel-to-reel tape machine and some of the best craft cocktails in the Cities. Reservations are a virtual necessity at Young Joni, and nearby street parking is available.

165 Thirteenth Ave. NE, Minneapolis
612-345-5719
youngjoni.com

ZEN BOX IZAKAYA

Zen Box Izakaya upends your notions of Japanese dining. There's no sushi on the menu. Nor will you dine Benihana-style seated around a knife-wielding chef who grills your food and flips it to your plate with a showy flourish. If your experience of Japanese beverages has been limited to sake or Sapporo beer, hold onto your cocktail glass.

An izakaya is a gathering place that serves food and drinks, with an atmosphere much like the bar on the old TV show *Cheers*, "where everybody knows your name." But instead of shouting out "Norm!," kamikaze headband-wearing staffers at Zen Box greet diners with a welcoming "Irasshaimase!" You may not notice it, but as you're feasting Zen Box takes you to a deeper level of Japanese culture than the more Americanized Japanese eateries usually offer.

The concept here is food-based social interaction, and there's no better way to do that than to sit down elbow-to-elbow and tuck into the Japanese comfort food that is this restaurant's specialty. "We cook what's seasonal and food that we love to eat," says Lina Goh, who owns Zen Box with her husband, John Ng. The star at Zen Box is ramen. It bears no resemblance to the cheap, dried version you ate late at night in college. "Ramen is Japan's soul food," says Goh. Ng and Goh have tramped the width and breadth of Japan to become ramen aficionados of the first rank. Try tonkotsu, for example, which is a ramen classic made with pork bone broth, fresh noodles, egg, seaweed, pickled ginger, and other ingredients. Look for weekend ramen specials, available only in limited quantities.

Because the kitchen is open to the dining room, you can watch the cooks prepare your meal. That might include takoyak, battered octopus with Japanese mayo. There's sashimi (like sushi without the rice) and a range of sautéed and fried dishes, such as the chicken kara-age, Japanese-style fried chicken served with Kamikaze sauce.

The Zen Box cocktail list contains standard cocktails, yes, but go for those with a Japanese twist. There's an extensive list of sake, Japanese beer, and whiskey and a selection of shochu, a vodka-like liquor made from rice and served ice cold or on the rocks. At Zen

Top right: The Zen Box menu features a wide array of Japanese dishes as well as its specialty, ramen. Photo by Travis Anderson

Above left: John Ng and Lina Goh. Photo by Travis Anderson

Above right: Zen Box Izakaya creates the atmosphere of a neighborhood eatery in Japan. Photo by Travis Anderson

Box, bartenders serve chu-hai cocktails, which are drinks typical to izakayas that combine fresh juice, syrups, and liqueurs.

Watch the Zen Box Facebook page for special pop up events it hosts during the year.

602 S. Washington Ave., Minneapolis
612-332-3936
zenbox.com

RESTAURANTS A-Z

112 Eatery
112 N. Third St.
Minneapolis

5-8 Club
5800 Cedar Ave. S.
Minneapolis

Alma
528 University Ave. SE
Minneapolis

Al's Breakfast
413 Fourteenth Ave. SE
Minneapolis

Babani's Kurdish Restaurant
32 Fillmore Ave. E.
St. Paul

Bachelor Farmer
50 N. Second Ave.
Minneapolis

Betty Danger's Country Club
2501 Marshall St. NE
Minneapolis

Big Daddy's BBQ
625 University Ave. W.
St. Paul

Birchwood Café
3311 E. Twenty-Fifth St.
Minneapolis

Bread & Pickle
4135 W. Lake Harriet Pkwy.
Minneapolis

Breaking Bread Café
1210 W. Broadway Ave.
Minneapolis

Brit's Pub and Eating
    Establishment
1110 Nicollet Mall
Minneapolis

Broders' Cucina Italiana
2308 W. Fiftieth St.
Minneapolis

Broders' Pasta Bar
5000 Penn Ave. S.
Minneapolis

Broders' Terzo
2221 W. Fiftieth St.
Minneapolis

Bryant-Lake Bowl
810 W. Lake St.
Minneapolis

Butcher & the Boar
1121 Hennepin Ave.
Minneapolis

Can Can Wonderland
755 Prior Ave. N.
St. Paul

Cecil's Deli
651 S. Cleveland Ave.
St. Paul

Chef Shack Ranch
3025 E. Franklin Ave.
Minneapolis

Chimborazo
2851 Central Ave. NE
Minneapolis

Como Dockside
1360 Lexington Pkwy. N.
St. Paul

Commodore Bar and
    Restaurant
79 Western Ave. N.
St. Paul

Cook St. Paul
1124 Payne Ave.
St. Paul

Cookie Cart
1119 W. Broadway Ave.
Minneapolis

Cooks of Crocus Hill
877 Grand Ave.
St. Paul

Cossetta Alimentari
211 Seventh St. W.
St. Paul

Costa Blanca Bistro
2416 Central Ave. NE
Minneapolis

Dakota Jazz Club and
    Restaurant
1010 Nicollet Ave.
Minneapolis

Dari-ette Drive-In
1440 Minnehaha Ave. E.
St. Paul

El Burrito Mercado
175 Cesar Chavez St. #2
St. Paul

Esker Grove
723 Vineland Place
Minneapolis

Fasika
510 Snelling Ave. N.
St. Paul

Fika
American Swedish Institute
2600 Park Ave.
Minneapolis

Forepaugh's Restaurant
276 S. Exchange St.
St. Paul

Gandhi Mahal
3009 Twenty-Seventh Ave. S.
Minneapolis

Gasthof zur Gemütlichkeit
2300 University Ave. NE
Minneapolis

Glam Doll Donuts
2605 Nicollet Ave. S.
519 Central Ave. NE
Minneapolis

Gyst Fermentation Bar
25 E. Twenty-Sixth St.
Minneapolis

Handsome Hog
203 E. Sixth St.
St. Paul

Happy Gnome
498 Selby Ave.
St. Paul

Herbivorous Butcher
507 First Ave. NE
Minneapolis

Hi-Lo Diner
4020 E. Lake St.
Minneapolis

Hola Arepa
3501 Nicollet Ave. S.
Minneapolis

Holy Land
2513 Central Ave. NE
Minneapolis

Ingebretsen's
1601 E. Lake St.
Minneapolis

Izzy's Ice Cream
1100 Second St.
Minneapolis

Jax Café
1928 University Ave.
Minneapolis

Kenwood
2115 W. Twenty-First St.
Minneapolis

Kitchen Window
in Calhoun Square
3001 Hennepin Ave.
Minneapolis

Kramarczuk's Sausage
  Company
215 E. Hennepin Ave.
Minneapolis

Lexington
1096 Grand Ave.
St. Paul

Matt's Bar
3500 Cedar Ave. S.
Minneapolis

Merlins Rest Pub
3601 E. Lake St.
Minneapolis

Meritage
410 Saint Peter St.
St. Paul

Mickey's Diner
36 W. Seventh St.
St. Paul

Midtown Global Market
920 E. Lake St.
Minneapolis

Milkjam Creamery
2743 Lyndale Ave. S.
Minneapolis

Mill City Farmers' Market
704 Second St.
Minneapolis

Minnesota State Fair
Minnesota State Fairgrounds
1265 Snelling Ave. N.
St. Paul

Minneapolis Farmers' Market
312 E. Lyndale Ave. N.
Minneapolis

Moscow on the Hill
371 Selby Ave.
St. Paul

Murray's
26 S. Sixth St.
Minneapolis

On's Kitchen
1613 University Ave.
St. Paul

Patisserie 46
4552 Grand Ave. S.
Minneapolis

Pimento
2524 Nicollet Ave. S.
Minneapolis

PinKU Japanese Street Food
20 University Ave.
Minneapolis

Psycho Suzi's Motor Lounge
1900 Marshall St. NE
Minneapolis

Quang
2719 Nicollet Ave. S.
Minneapolis

Reverie Café
1931 Nicollet Ave. S.
Minneapolis

Revival
4257 Nicollet Ave.
Minneapolis

Rose Street Patisserie
2811 W. Forty-Third St.
Minneapolis

Safari
3010 Fourth Ave. S.
Minneapolis

Saint Dinette
261 E. Fifth St.
St. Paul

Saint Genevieve
5003 Bryant Ave. S.
Minneapolis

St. Paul Farmers' Market
290 E. Fifth St.
Saint Paul

Saint Paul Grill
350 Market St.
St. Paul

Salty Tart
in Midtown Global Market
920 E. Lake St.
Minneapolis

Sea Change
806 S. Second St.
Minneapolis

Sea Salt
4825 Minnehaha Ave.
Minneapolis

Sioux Chef
612-486-2433

Sparks
230 Cedar Lake Rd. S.
Minneapolis

Spoon and Stable
211 N. First St.
Minneapolis

Surly Destination Brewery
520 Malcolm Ave. SE
Minneapolis

Tin Fish
3000 E. Calhoun Pkwy.
Minneapolis

Tiny Diner
1024 E. Thirty-Eighth St.
Minneapolis

Tongue in Cheek
989 Payne Ave.
St. Paul

Tori Ramen
161 Victoria St. N.
St. Paul

Travail Kitchen and
   Amusements
4124 W. Broadway Ave.
Robbinsdale

Tullibee
300 Washington Ave.
Minneapolis

United Noodles and Unideli
2015 E. Twenty-Fourth St.
Minneapolis

Victor's 1959 Café
3756 Grand Ave. S.
Minneapolis

Victory 44
2203 N. Forty-Fourth Ave.
Minneapolis

Volstead's Emporium
711 Lake St.
Minneapolis

W. A. Frost and Company
374 Selby Ave.
St. Paul

World Street Kitchen
2743 Lyndale Ave. S.
Minneapolis

Young Joni
165 Thirteenth Ave. NE
Minneapolis

Zen Box Izakaya
602 S. Washington Ave.
Minneapolis

APPENDIX